BANGLADESH WAR

REPORT FROM GROUND ZERO

Manash Ghosh

PAPER MISSILE
NIYOGI BOOKS

Published by
NIYOGI BOOKS
Block D, Building No. 77,
Okhla Industrial Area, Phase-I,
New Delhi-110 020, INDIA
Tel: 91-11-26816301, 26818960
Email: niyogibooks@gmail.com
Website: www.niyogibooksindia.com

Editor: Sucharita Ghosh
Design: Shashi Bhushan Prasad
Cover design: Pinaki De

ISBN: 978-93-91125-37-0
Publication: 2021

Printed at: Niyogi Offset Pvt. Ltd., New Delhi, India

Dedicated to valiant Muktijoddhas *and bravehearts of the Indian Army who fought shoulder to shoulder to realize Sheikh Mujib's dream of founding a secular and democratic Bengali nation*

CONTENTS

FOREWORD

Manash Ghosh's steadfast and unwavering commitment to stand by the defenceless and persecuted Bengalis of former East Pakistan led to this book. It impelled him to report, disregarding grave danger to his personal life, the mass slaughter of Bengalis by the Pakistani military in its bid to deny them the fruits of an overwhelming electoral verdict. He was swayed by their uncompromising fight, led by their unquestioned leader Sheikh Mujibur Rahman, to attain political independence and economic freedom for themselves. Manash Ghosh was the first foreign journalist to enter erstwhile East Pakistan to report the mayhem that the Pakistan military had unleashed on unarmed Bengalis while executing 'Operation Searchlight'. He also happened to be the first foreign journalist to report on the valiant popular resistance that all sections of the Bengali society had put up against the ruthless Pakistani onslaught of which the world was then totally unaware. His reporting on the Jessore resistance on 30 March 1971 in *The Statesman* with telltale war photographs bear testimony to this fact. It was this reporting which brought international journalists like Peter Hazelhurst of *The Times*, London, and Martin Woollacott of *The Guardian* post-haste to Calcutta to report on the freedom struggle being waged by the Bengalis. His reporting from Chuadanga and Pabna in the first week of April was also a pathbreaking journalistic exercise. No other foreign journalist had dared to go so deep inside the Pakistani territory which had already come to be known as Bangladesh. He was one of the very few Indian journalists who had covered the liberation war from start to finish and whose reports from the front were given due weightage by the Indian policy planners in Delhi and also by the Calcutta-based Tajuddin Ahmed-led government in exile which factored his news reports into their decision-making while strategizing the conduct of the *muktijuddho*.

Well before the war started, Manash Ghosh was the first among journalists who wrote an article in *The Sunday Statesman* predicting what was going to happen in East Pakistan. Even after Bangladesh came into being his respect for democratic aspirations of the Bengalis did not wane or flinch a bit. After Bangabandhu Sheikh Mujib's assassination whenever the military regime derailed or banished democracy from Bangladesh, he used his mighty pen to fight for the restoration of democracy in our country. This ensured that he was persona non grata in successive regimes of General Ziaur Rahman and General Ershad. He was blacklisted even by a democratically elected Prime Minister Begum Zia. She did not like his writings criticizing her government's policies to promote Islamic jihad and for highlighting her close ties with the Pakistani military regime led by General Parvez Musharraf. He was denied a visa for eight years as he was told bluntly by Bangladeshi diplomats that he was not welcome to their country for his anti-government writings. It was this uncompromising stance which earned him the respect and admiration of the Bengali leadership and masses. This transformed his image from that of a mere Indian journalist into 'our very own Manashda'. In Bangladesh everyone from highly placed leaders, academics, to the man on the street address him by this honorific title.

Manash Ghosh's reporting from various battlefronts like Jessore, Chuadanga, Pabna, the Ganga (near the Sarda police academy in

Rajshahi), Garibpur and Khulna are the most enlivening parts of this book, setting it apart from others of its genre. It highlights how the Indian generals like Shahbeg Singh, Sujan Singh Oban, who raised and trained the Mukti Bahini, transformed in a matter of weeks thousands of unlettered Bengali youth, mostly from the peasant stock, into highly motivated and much dreaded guerrilla fighters who struck terror in the hearts of the Pakistan military. He has also documented the dedication and valour of Bangladeshi commanders, who led from the front with very little fire power, and the critical role of men in daring operations. Names like Captain Rafiqul Islam, Major Khaled Mosharraf, A.T.M. Hyder, Abu Osman Chowdhury, Captain Hafizuddin, all of whom fought like tigers, and their heroic roles are well chronicled in this book.

The highlight of this book is the compelling narrative of how Bangabandhu, impelled by the ruling military junta's exploitative and discriminatory policies pursued towards the Bengali people, gradually inspired them to wage a liberation war with Indian help and win freedom. It took him years of planning and strategization in order to achieve this goal. Over three decades he liaised with three successive Indian prime ministers. Very few Indian journalists have written with such insight, depth and passion as Manash Ghosh has done. He has recounted many unknown and unpublished episodes which have lent colour and lustre to the book. Since he had a ringside view of the *muktijuddho* he has sequentially chronicled its progress and setbacks including its numerous twists and turns.

Another fascinating aspect of this book is that the author recounts many anecdotes in easy storytelling form, having gone deep inside Bangladesh to cover the war and being on excellent terms with the government in exile leaders and sector commanders of the Mukti Bahini. This book also succinctly recounts the adverse reaction of a section of the Indian political spectrum and of a particular community to Mrs Gandhi's unequivocal support to the *muktijuddho*. All in all, this book is a prized offering on the centenary year of Bangabandhu's birth and completion of 50 years of Bangladesh's independence. *Joy Bangla*!

Dr Muntassir Mamoon
Bangabandhu professor, Chittagong University
President of 1971: Genocide Torture and Archives Museum Trust
Dhaka

PREFACE
A STORY FORETOLD

I am still not sure whether it was my reporter's intuition – I was just a cub reporter at *The Statesman*, Calcutta then – or sheer providence that saw me attending the Second Asian Highway Car Rally on the morning of 15 November 1970 at the India-East Pakistan border at Petrapole-Benapole. This rally from Tehran to Dacca, was being organized by a UN body, the Economic Commission for Asia and the Far East (ECAFE), and was taking place four days after the catastrophic cyclone that had struck the southern deltaic region of East Pakistan.

That turned out to be the most rewarding day of my journalistic career.

The cyclone had claimed over 500,000 human lives and had caused incalculable destruction of property. More importantly, the car rally provided me with the most fascinating insight, invaluable to any reporter, into the tumultuous developments that had been set in motion in East Pakistan for the next one year. I had the proud privilege of covering them for *The Statesman* for the entire period.

My initiation into the coverage of the Liberation War and my subsequent three-year posting in Dacca in an independent Bangladesh was somewhat unconventional and dramatic. The 60 participants in their cars of various makes heading for Dacca that day paled into insignificance when I caught the chitchat between the Bengalis from the other side of the border, in what was considered to be no man's land. I did not know them but eavesdropping into their conversation was mesmerizing. For me, that was more intriguing than the harrowing tales of the rallyists, who had driven all the way down from Tehran to the Indian border town, Bongaon.

I got talking to the three Bengali strangers. Great talkers, as most Bengalis are, they chronicled for me the events on their own – from Field Marshal Ayub Khan's downfall, caused mostly by a mass upheaval in East Pakistan, to General Yahya Khan's rise to power, and Sheikh Mujib's six-point autonomy movement – which had overwhelmed the Bengali mind in the country's eastern province in the preceding months.

The trio's cogently argued narrative was laced with such credible interpretation of events that, initially, I thought they were seasoned politicians. The ensuing tumult in the region proved how prescient they were. I asked them point blank whether they were from Sheikh Mujib's Awami League. Their immediate riposte was 'Every Bengali today, whether Muslim, Hindu or Buddhist, in East Pakistan, is a committed follower of Sheikh Mujib and his Awami League.' The trio grabbed the opportunity to befriend me when I told them that I was a reporter from *The Statesman*, Calcutta.

They were cautious though. Prior to opening up, they had given me a bit of a shock when they somewhat apologetically asked me for my official identity card saying 'We want to be absolutely sure who you are.' Unused to having my identity questioned, I reluctantly showed them my ID card and the change was instantaneous: 'Now we can talk to you freely,' they said as they predicted the shape of things to come in their province. They would not disclose their identities though.

Only one gave me his name and let on that he worked in the Jessore collectorate as an assistant secretary and he belonged to the provincial civil service. The other two were tougher nuts to crack. I got the feeling from the tenor of their talk that they were from the intelligence wing of the police and the land customs. I was taken aback by the effusiveness of the Bengali nationalist spirit; their enthusiastic support for Sheikh Mujib; and that they were not worried about talking to an Indian; a total stranger at that. Their spontaneity struck me as very un-Pakistani and politically incorrect.

By the Pakistani yardstick they were blatantly blasphemous and treacherous. Understandably, I was hesitant to open up to them because they were Pakistani nationals. My sixth sense warned me that the trio was perhaps laying a trap for me. Yet there was something about their effusive regard for *The Statesman*, of which they were ardent and loyal readers. As most Bengalis of my era, they took special pride in proclaiming that they had learnt English by reading the paper daily. Between the three they managed to break down my resistance, especially when they told me the assistant secretary and the land customs officer got smuggled copies of the paper delivered to their office table in Jessore every morning.

An 'in' into *The Statesman* meant something special to them and I quickly realized that their purpose of befriending me had much to do with sensitizing me about the plight of India's eastern neighbour and the mood of the Bengali in East Pakistan. They frankly confessed that they were baffled by an average Indian's (including mine) abysmal ignorance of what was happening in one wing of the next-door neighbouring country. They complained that despite successive mass political upheavals in East Pakistan in 1969, the Indian media, including All India Radio, preferred to ignore them.

I soon realized that they were deliberately providing me with the necessary news feed so that I could write about it in *The Statesman*, especially about the impending elections, in which the Sheikh Mujib-led Awami League was 100 per cent certain to make a clean sweep in East Pakistan. Those were the days when there was no official flow of news, people and goods from West Bengal or any other part of India to East Pakistan and vice versa. Indian reporters wanting to visit Dacca were first required to travel to West Pakistan from where, after proper and intensive screening, they were allowed to fly to Dacca.

Getting a Pakistani visa was impossible for any Indian. So most developments there went unreported. News agency reports from Dacca were short and sketchy and few and far between. They did not meet the appetite for news in those who were actually interested in what was happening across our side of the border. *The Statesman* carried dispatches filed by Peter Hazelhurst, the South Asia correspondent of *The Times*, London from Dacca once in a while. The reports belonged to the play-safe brand of journalism. Anyone reporting the brutal truth would have his or her visa cancelled.

Thus, while the rally cars were slowly rolling into East Pakistan one by one and heading for Dacca, amidst honking of horns and cheering from bystanders, I received my first-hand initiation into the gruesome developments that were to follow, but not before the Bengalis under Sheikh Mujib would show their western counterparts that they would not take things lying down.

The trio had prepared me for the results at the hustings, when the country went to polls on 7 December but not for the bloody denouement that would follow.

The Alienation

Never in the recent history of liberation wars did a natural disaster trigger such popular upheaval as it did in East Pakistan. The upheaval snowballed into Bangladesh's Liberation War, leading to the break-up of Pakistan. The inept handling of the 11 November 1970 cyclone, which hit the southern coast of East Pakistan – amongst the worst natural disasters of modern times – by the Pakistani military junta, not only exposed the deep fissures between West and East Pakistan but also reinforced and widened them to such an extent that they eventually became unbridgeable. The two wings of Pakistan were torn asunder.

The devastating cyclone lashed the southern coastline at a speed of 190 km per hour, accompanied by tidal waves 13-20 ft high. It swept away 500,000 people to sea and left in its wake a massive trail of death, destruction and human misery. The entire southern coast was in a shambles. Rotting bodies of humans and cattle lay strewn all around as none came to bury them. There was not a single survivor on 13 islands near the Chittagong coast. Almost 50 per cent of the 16,76,000 people living in Tazumuddin Island died. Those who survived were as good as dead without food, drinking water or a shelter over their heads. Their plight was exacerbated by the military junta, which wilfully denied timely relief for them. As a result, apart from the 500,000 people who had perished in the disaster, almost an equal number was added to the list of victims suffering from cyclone-related morbidity. Of the 77,000 on-shore fishermen, only 31,000 survived. Livestock perished too; nearly 200,000 cattle died.

Unperturbed by these developments, the Pakistani president, General Yahya Khan, chose not to come and oversee relief operations. Instead he continued with his role of facilitating Henry Kissinger's secret trip to China. To him helping Nixon and Mao reach a rapprochement was of greater priority than lessening the mounting distress of cyclone survivors. Because that would help him to be on the right side of the two world leaders. The general Bengali mass and joint opposition of East Pakistan accused the military junta of showing 'criminal indifference' to their misery. They accused Yahya of unleashing a man-made catastrophe that could easily have been avoided. Sheikh Mujib was at the vanguard of this campaign. He and his trusted lieutenants moved from village to village in the affected areas, distributing relief and providing solace to the affected. With his first-hand knowledge and experience of what the cyclone survivors were undergoing, he made the Pakistan establishment's 'Himalayan neglect and deprivation' of the Bengalis of East Pakistan his main electoral campaign plank. This provided the decisive electoral edge to his party, the Awami League, in the coming parliamentary and provincial assembly elections.

The storm warning system in East Pakistan, the Opposition alleged, was inadequate to begin with and improperly used. Although the cyclone had formed over the central Bay of Bengal on 3 November and had intensified while moving northward in the next eight days, there was no proper tracking of its movement. The Pakistan Meteorological Office only signalled for 'danger preparedness'. The 'great danger' signal 'was belatedly hoisted and broadcast only on the day the cyclone made landfall'. This was because the Pakistan Meteorological Department had suddenly discontinued the time-tested practice of letting the people know well in advance through the media about the impending natural disasters that would hit any part of the country. When the Pak Met department realized that the tropical cyclone would be of a devastating nature, it decided to issue only a 'cautionary signal', almost at the eleventh hour. It was criminally late. Yahya, cornered by the international press for mishandling the disaster, admitted to a 'lack of understanding of the magnitude of the cyclone disaster in time'. However, he strongly disapproved of Mujib's strategy of using the cyclone issue as 'political football' for spreading disaffection and garnering votes to gain electoral advantage.

Historically, the southern coast of Bay of Bengal has been buffeted by tropical cyclones. In October 1960, it faced two destructive cyclones, one after another, which killed nearly 20,000 people. Yet, no cyclone shelters had been built on high grounds for residents to seek refuge at times of such natural catastrophe. Those who survived the 1970 cyclone suffered such serious abrasions on their chests and hands for tightly holding on to tree trunks that many later died of septicemia. The Hurricane Center of the US Government had made a detailed study of the pattern of cyclones that periodically hit East Pakistan and made recommendations that were ignored.

The recommendations included the setting up of a sophisticated early warning system. Since implementation of those recommendations would mean a large capital investment by the Pakistan government, they were put on the backburner. Thus the latest assault of the tidal seawater had befouled all the fresh water sources, forcing survivors to drink polluted water for over a month. Such transgressions of the Yahya regime had deepened the anger, mistrust and pent-up frustration of the Bengali masses, which translated into a massive mandate for the Awami League in the 7 December general election.

Much of what the trio had said at the car rally revolved around the devastating cyclone and its 'cocksure negative and decisive impact' on the election result. The '*paschimas*' (the Bengalis' derisive name for the West Punjabis), had a false sense of racial superiority that had heavily prejudiced their thinking and affected their decision-making pertaining to the Bengalis of East Pakistan. Fiercely protective of their mother tongue, the Bengalis realized how Urdu was 'being cleverly foisted' on them. My companions pointed out: 'Look at this Urdu welcome sign, "*khoshamded*"[welcome], written in Bengali script that greets visitors entering East Pakistan at this no man's land. We wanted "*Swagatam*" to be written but it was considered too much of a Hindu welcome sign and was rejected. This is the natural outcome of the policy of deliberate discrimination that the Pakistani ruling establishment, mainly controlled by Punjabis, follow towards their 75 million so-called Bengali Muslim brethren.'

The trio talked about the cyclone victims being asked to fend for themselves even though there were dozens of foreign aircraft carrying relief items landing at the Dacca airport every day and unloading their cargo. Surprisingly, they were being stacked at the airport's cargo shed and godowns in Dacca. Worse, the expensive relief items were being flown to West Pakistan on the plea that '*garib, ghatiya*' (poor and sub-standard) Bengalis were not used to them.

The customs officer said that he had seen stacks and stacks of cargo 'at the Benapole land cargo godown' that morning. 'I saw large stocks of Indian relief items lying stacked right up to the ceiling but not being distributed.' The reason was simple. Yahya wanted neither India's image nor goodwill to improve significantly among the Bengalis of East Pakistan by the distribution of Indian relief items among them. He deliberately deployed fewer men in the affected areas and the Indian items remained locked in godowns while the victims were told that enough relief teams were not available to distribute them.

My new friends explained that President Yahya Khan was not interested in visiting the devastated areas and meeting the victims because he was keen to build bridges between the Nixon administration and Mao Zedong's Communist China as Nixon's wingman. He had twice postponed his Dacca plans because of his 'foreign commitment'. The assistant secretary said that the brigade commander of the Jessore garrison, a certain Brigadier Rahim Durrani, had used a specious plea for not rushing his brigade to the affected areas of Bhola for lack of public transport. Elsewhere he had argued that military vehicles could not be used for civilian relief work.

Underscoring the point about discrimination, the assistant secretary quoted from a conversation that his boss, the Jessore collector, a Punjabi Civil Service of Pakistan (CSP) officer, had with a junior fellow Punjabi civil servant, who was pressing him hard to go by the provisions of the rule book for requisitioning the services of the Jessore garrison in aid of the civil administration. 'The reply of the collector was a revelation of how the Punjabi mind worked towards the Bengalis,' said the assistant secretary. 'The junior officer was too ashamed to recount to me the exact conversation but told me, "You know how we Punjabis describe you Bengalis as '*kala, nata*' [dark and short] people", who "deserved only despise and no empathy"'. In fact, the collector had asked the junior officer why was he so concerned about the plight of the cyclone victims. Eventually, the Jessore brigade reached Bhola almost three weeks after the devastation.

There was much more by way of complaint against the West Pakistan regime. A shortage of helicopters was hampering relief work as the bulk of Pakistan's helicopter fleet was stationed in West Pakistan. The eastern wing had just three, which could not cope with the magnitude of the relief operations, they said. Offers to rush helicopters by other countries (including India) had been brusquely spurned by President Yahya who said: 'Pakistan had enough of them as well as other resources to manage relief work on its own.' India's special gesture of extending extra overflying facility to Pakistan so that it could ferry additional helicopters from West to East was similarly dismissed.

A Gathering Storm

The trio was clear: 'Our destiny will change and we can see it as clear as daylight. A severe storm is gathering on Pakistan's political horizon; if the elections are free and fair, the electoral verdict will help the storm gain momentum and the tidal wave of Bengali nationalism will drown the very concept of Pakistan. Mark our words, on this day of the highway rally, and recall them after the poll results are out. Not even India will escape the fury of that storm. It is going to unsettle you as well.' I did not realize that every word they spoke that day would turn into reality so soon.

We parted; they were hopeful that their story would be of use to me. 'If you have any doubt about our credibility and the authenticity of our observations, cross-check it with our ace and legendary swimmer Brojen Das who is now in Calcutta.' Brojen, a legendary figure and a recipient of Pakistan's highest award for sportsmen, had wide contacts in Pakistan's top civil and military echelons. He was close to the Awami League too and very well informed. I was given his Calcutta hotel address and its telephone number. They insisted that I see him on my return to the city.

I did; the very next day, early in the morning. I met Brojen Das in his very modest room at a Bowbazar hotel and told him about my meeting with the trio at the rally. From my description of them, he recognized them instantly and called them his 'very close friends'. All of them were his classmates in school and university and had remained in close contact with one another. The customs officer was an assistant collector and the police officer was the deputy superintendent of police, Jessore range. Brojen Das confirmed every word that they had said.

I asked why had they risked their lives and careers by talking to an Indian reporter and telling him things that were blatantly anti-Pakistan in nature. Das explained: 'My fellow Bengalis of all religions are smarting under tremendous humiliation. The grave injustice of every conceivable kind that they have to endure daily has turned them against the concept of Pakistan. You wait and see what happens in the election. There will be an implosion in the ballot box on 7 December.' He also suggested that I interview the Indian participants in the rally, especially the Bengalis, on their return home and find out the kind of warm welcome they had received from the Bengalis on their way to and in Dacca.

I rushed to the office and narrated my experience to my immediate bosses and expressed the wish to write an article. I was stoutly rebuked for going to the border 'without clearance' and indulging in 'professional adventurism'. I was also told that I was 'too junior [a mere cub reporter] and not qualified enough' to handle an international story of this nature. But I did not lose heart. I strategized instead. If the news and editorial pages of *The Statesman* did not allow my piece, I would try to get it printed in the paper's 'Sunday Magazine' section. I was told I could try my luck with the section in-charge, Sunanda K. Datta-Ray, *The Statesman's* most illustrious and youngest assistant editor. He was held in such high esteem that it was inconceivable for a junior-most cub reporter like me to approach him.

The Statesman's hierarchical style of functioning also came in my way. The corridor on the second floor of the majestic Statesman House, where he sat in a sprawling room, was almost out of bounds for someone like me. I had, however, gathered from the deputy chief reporter, Muralijiban Ghosh, that Datta-Ray's ancestors hailed from Brahmanbaria in East Pakistan and that he had a soft corner for the people across the border and was interested in happenings on the other side.

I summoned enough courage to make a telephone call to him and, with a lot of trepidation, sought an appointment. I addressed him as Sunanda da and asked if he could spare me a few minutes as I had very interesting details on the current mood and happenings in East Pakistan. I told him that I wanted to write an article in the magazine section. He asked if I could go and see him right away. When I entered his room, he asked me, 'What's happening in East Pakistan that you so desperately want to write about?'

I recounted the narrative of the trio and said I had cross-checked the facts with the record-breaking English Channel swimmer, Brojen Das, currently in Calcutta, who had vouched for the story's authenticity. Datta-Ray said that it could be 'an interesting piece in the wake of the cyclone and its mishandling by Yahya'. He asked if the piece was ready and how long it was. The next words filled me with great excitement. 'I will hold over the scheduled piece and make yours the next Sunday's cover story. But keep your piece confined to what the Indian rallyists said about their experiences in East Pakistan.'

I told him that my piece would be quite big and I was waiting for the Indians, especially, the Calcutta-based rallyists, to return from Dacca. 'So then I am scheduling yours for Sunday, after next.' It was worth the wait. The Indian participants had a cold and almost hostile reception in West Pakistan, where they were constantly tailed by plainclothesmen. They were expecting more of the same in Dacca. What they found was the warmest of embraces as if they were long-lost cousins reuniting in strange circumstances.

Wherever the Indian rallyists stopped their cars, they were surrounded by curious crowds asking if they spoke Bengali. Mahandra Lalwani, who won the first prize among the 60 odd rallyists, was frequently asked, '*Aapni ki Bangla boltey paren*?' (Can you speak Bengali?) He was cheered when he said in his broken Bengali, '*Bujhte pari boltey parina*' (I can understand but not speak). They were overwhelmed by the lavishness of the hospitality; their cars were stopped on the way to recharge them with plenty of *daaber pani* (coconut water). Some among the crowd would clamber up the roadside coconut trees in a jiffy and throw down clumps of green coconut, which were cut and served to the rallyists to drink.

Once in Dacca, the local Bengalis called on them in their hotel rooms and took them out for lunch and dinner to Dacca's famous Chinese restaurants. Those who were fish-eaters were taken to old Dacca's famed hotels and restaurants to be treated to delectable varieties of *maacher jhol*. The hosts rued the fact that the Pakistani rulers had deliberately planned and ensured that there should be a total disconnect between the Bengalis on both sides of the border. They also lamented that they were not allowed to visit the city of their dream, Calcutta, because of West Pakistan's hatred for India and the Bengalis.

What the rallyists found extraordinary was that every word their Dacca hosts spoke resonated with Bengali nationalist spirit. They were overwhelmed by the craze for Calcutta. Those who had studied in Calcutta schools and colleges were curious to know about their current state. Calcutta was the magnet but if they visited the Indian Deputy High Commission in Dacca for a visa to visit Calcutta, the Pakistani security would hound them day and night and ask them all kinds of questions to harass them no end. This forced many to cancel their visits to Calcutta.

They yearned to see Bengali movies and buy the works of Tagore, Tarasankar, Buddhadeb Bose, Samaresh Bose and, of course, the collected works of other famous Bengali authors from the other shore of Bengal. Import and screening of Bengali and Hindi films were completely banned as the Pakistani rulers discouraged any cultural affinity between the Bengalis and Indians. The locals were tired of reading the pirated editions of Bengali novels by Indian authors. The Pakistani customs seized all Bengali books that they tried to smuggle in their baggage. Hunger for Bengali films, especially Ray's Apu trilogy, was so great that those who went to London, Singapore or America came back with reels of those films for private viewing at home for close family, friends and relatives. What the rallyists experienced during their stay in East Pakistan added substantial meat and substance to my 4,000-word article that pleased Datta-Ray.

The headline that Datta-Ray gave, 'When Brother meets Brother', made the article an even more compelling read. The day it appeared, the joint news editor of *Jugantar*, Anil Bhattacharjee, an old Pakistan hand, who had covered General Ayub Khan's presidential election in 1965 and had travelled with Ayub during his whistle-stop campaign in East Pakistan as his special invitee, dropped in at the Statesman House to find out who Manash Ghosh was. He did not know me, a new entrant to *The Statesman's* reporters' room. When he did meet me, he was effusive in his praise: '*Tumi kamal korey diyecho* [you have done wonders] by correctly and objectively portraying East Pakistan's fast evolving political and social situation. I did not realize that you were so young. Keep an eye on East Pakistan, my boy. Because, my sources say, many earth-shaking things are going to happen there in the coming months. You have given an inkling of them in your article.'

I received so many congratulatory telephone calls that day that I had lost count of them. One was from *Amrita Bazar Patrika's* retired special correspondent, Kalipada Biswas, who was well known for his knowledge of East Pakistan affairs. He wanted to meet me at the Press Club that evening. There he embraced me with open arms and said my extremely nuanced piece gave a clear projection of things to come. He agreed that the coming election would be a turning point in Pakistan's history. He found my piece lucid as it brought out the mood of the Muslim Bengalis. He advised me to keep my ears and eyes open on events in East Pakistan.

I religiously listened to the Bengali broadcasts of BBC and VOA, which kept me somewhat abreast of day-to-day developments across the border, though I realized that they were sketchy at best. Both the US and British governments supported the Pakistani military establishment. They considered Mujib to be India's proxy in East Pakistan, who wanted to break up the Islamic state. I also got almost daily feedback from Brojen Das on Mujib's and his Awami League's prospects in the election. Every time I met him he gave me the thumbs up sign to convey the message that everything was going along expected lines. I did not know what his sources of information were but that he was getting the right feedback was proved by subsequent events.

One day he shared his great concern: 'I am very doubtful about Yahya allowing a free and fair election. The day the military and the Punjabi ruling establishment know the poll outcome for sure, they will rescind the entire poll process. The only thing that could hold them back from indulging in such a misadventure would be the fear of a violent and popular backlash that such a regressive step would unleash on East Pakistan.' About the same time I discovered that there was another source, a close Hindu confidant of Mujib, Chittaranjan Sutar, from Barisal who had been sent to Calcutta by Sheikh Mujib well ahead of the 1970 election, to liaise with the government of India on his behalf.

He was Mujib's personal pointsman in India. He had settled down in a large house in Bhowanipore's middle-class neighbourhood at 43, Rajendra Road, Northern Park area. His house, Sunny Villa, had turned into a beehive of Awami League activists in Calcutta. Anyone coming from Dacca or elsewhere in Bangladesh and trying to meet Indian leaders or officers had to have his clearance. Without his nod, no Indian would entertain anyone but more on this later.

Ambivalent India

For me, the next three weeks, until the elections were held, were very agonizing indeed. There were reports of the massive turnouts at Sheikh Mujib's public meetings, where he urged the Bengalis of all creeds and religions to assert their pride and Bengali identity on the polling day through their votes. He urged them to vote to have the inequities of the past decisively undone. What struck me as a little strange was the total apathy of the educated Bengali middle class, especially the post-Partition refugees, now settled in Calcutta and in the rest of West Bengal, to the developments on the other side of the border.

Many even rebuked me for my unnecessary interest in the affairs of East Pakistan that, to their minds, should be of no concern to any Indian. They were yet to get over the hangover of atrocities, persecution and indignities during the pre- and post-Partition riots. Their common refrain was '…let them stew in their own juices. How can we forget the horrendous things that they did to us?' I was accused of being *ghoti* (man from West Bengal, as opposed to those who came from East Bengal) and that too a 'Delhiwala' who was indifferent to their 'nightmarish experiences' that they could not 'forget or forgive or wish away'. The Left-leaning intellectuals of the pro-Moscow variety pursued the developments with great empathy and interest though. Even an East Pakistan refugee-centric party like the CPI(M) initially ignored the happenings as an 'internal and domestic matter' of Pakistan not warranting any special attention from the Indian communists.

The attitude of the Indian Press, especially of Calcutta's Bengali vernacular dailies, too, was bordering on indifference. Yet, while the initial events in East Pakistan got little or no attention and space in the media, developments in West Pakistan commanded a lot of space. This was partly because the Indian establishment, too, including the media, was largely influenced by the policies pursued by the Punjabi-dominated Pakistani establishment, driven by the logic that East Pakistan's defence lay in West Pakistan. This Indian establishment firmly believed that nothing earth-shaking was ever going to happen in East Pakistan that could be of any concern to India.

The Nehru era viewed East Pakistan as a harmless appendage of the West even though the then Pakistani leaders had already begun operationalizing their policy of inflicting a thousand cuts on India to bleed it white. They were harbouring Naga and Mizo rebels and their leaders, Z.A. Phizo and Brigadier Sailo, in the dense forests of Chittagong Hill Tracts (CHT). The dense CHT forests provided an excellent cover for these rebels, serving both as a hideout and a launch pad for carrying out large-scale insurgency operations in India's north-eastern states, especially in the adjoining Indian states of Nagaland and Mizoram. They were actively aided by the Pakistan military and the Chinese Communist Party; enjoying the protection of the Pakistani generals who had promoted Dacca as the first overseas political base and outpost for Naga and Mizo rebel outfits. From Dacca, the rebel leaders activated their foreign contacts and made frequent trips to Islamabad, Beijing and London and, occasionally, to the UN in New York to take their 'freedom struggle' global. The British missionary Reverend Michael Scott who championed the Naga Cause, visited Dacca whenever it suited him.

Yet, the Indian foreign office, apparently under Nehru's instruction – as told to me by the redoubtable Subimal Dutt, India's first high commissioner in Bangladesh and earlier the longest serving Indian foreign secretary – had downgraded the size and the operational importance of the Indian Deputy High Commission in Dacca such that it generally operated at less than half its sanctioned strength. Thus India could not effectively keep tabs on Indian insurgents in East Pakistan. The intelligence head of India's Dacca mission, B.C. Sinha, whom I met in Dacca in December 1971, had confirmed this as he lamented that he could not keep proper checks on the Naga and Mizo leaders, who lived in Dacca and Chittagong most of the time and openly moved around in flashy cars with Pakistani military escort. He lacked the manpower, resources and money to do the job. The Indian high commissioner based in Islamabad rarely visited Dacca to take stock of the evolving situation there.

India's policy makers in Delhi dealt with their counterparts in Pakistan's power centres, first in Karachi, then to 'Pindi' and, finally, Islamabad. They had to interact with them almost on a daily basis concerning issues involving both countries but events in the western wing stole the limelight in the Indian Press. Two wars on India's western front and an 'unquiet and live' western border, the Kashmir tangle, Indus water-sharing arrangement, to mention a few, contributed immensely to this lopsided news coverage. Moreover, there were more Bhatias, Dass, Malhotras, Chopras and Nayars in positions of authority in the Indian media, who originally hailed from West Pakistan and were extremely nostalgic about their alma maters, their homes in Lahore, Sialkot, Karachi, Pindi or Peshawar. They longed for their Muslim friends then occupying positions of authority in Pakistan's top hierarchy and with whom they could directly relate and converse freely with great ease. Bengalis were comparatively in the periphery both in the Indian political mainstream and in the media.

This was apparent to me not only on the basis of my personal experiences but also over conversations with my senior colleagues at *The Statesman* and elsewhere, as I tried to decode the prevailing Pakistani political and electoral scene. I sought help from *The Statesman's* Delhi's then resident editor, Kuldip Nayar, who had then just returned from a trip to Pakistan. He had written extensively on Zulfiqar Ali Bhutto and his People's Party's rising prospects in Pakistan's political and electoral firmament but made little or no mention of Sheikh Mujib and his Awami League's future prospects. When I tried to speak to him on the phone, his secretary asked me what exactly I did at the Calcutta *Statesman* and he promptly retorted that Mr Nayar had pressing engagements and did not talk to 'strangers' on a sensitive issue like Pakistani politics on the phone.

My attempts to reach Surinder Nihal Singh who, until a few years ago, was posted as *The Statesman's* Pakistan correspondent in Islamabad, also bore no fruit, largely because I was 'far too a junior to be speaking to someone of such seniority like him'. My queries to the under secretary of the Home Political department of the West Bengal government, who kept an eye on developments in East Pakistan on behalf of the state government, also drew a blank as the information he claimed was 'highly confidential and classified'. The only person who responded somewhat positively to my queries was Mr Golak Majumdar, inspector general of Border Security Force (BSF), Eastern Frontier.

Golak Majumdar spoke to me in his office and asked what I knew about the coming elections in East Pakistan. He complimented me for my 'perceptive' piece, and informed me that he had sent a copy of my article marked as 'must read' to his director general, K.F. Rustamji in Delhi. 'Your piece has, for the first time, put the alienation of East

Pakistan's educated Muslim Bengali middle class from their Punjabi-dominated Pakistani rulers, in Indian public domain. The way the trio, you mentioned in your article, sought you out in no man's land, and poured their hearts out to you is enough of an indication of the desperation of the people and decision makers on the other side.' He concurred with my assessment of the emerging electoral scene in East Pakistan, especially Sheikh Mujib's Awami League winning more than two third of Pakistan's National Assembly seats. Golak Majumdar first informed me about the totally different dimension that Pakistan's politics would assume after the elections.

'If Sheikh Mujib sweeps the poll with a decisive mandate, will the ruling Pakistani establishment, especially the military, hand over power to him and his Awami League? That is the million-dollar question.' The fact was that he and his party were considered *gaddars* or traitors by the West Pakistan establishment. Golak Majumdar directed me to 'try to find out something relevant from that angle'. My question was: 'Why would they allow the elections to be held in the first place knowing its outcome was a foregone conclusion?' He ruefully explained: 'The Pakistani rulers will not risk a virtual bloodbath that such a decision will certainly entail. But keep an eye on East Pakistan's evolving situation because whatever happens it will have an immediate and direct impact on our side. Unfortunately, the Calcutta Press is not alive to the situation.'

He went out of his way to point me towards his 'agile and well informed' Petrapole commandant, K.B. Singh, who got regular and reliable information from deep inside East Pakistan. I followed up Golak babu's suggestion by calling on Singh at his office at the Bongaon-Petrapole border. My brief interaction with K.B. Singh made it clear that the BSF's field units were bracing themselves for an unexpected turn of events in East Pakistan. Of late, the Bengali-speaking Pakistani police, customs and border guard officers posted at Benapole had been openly speaking to him about their disenchantment with Pakistani rulers, which was 'very unusual'.

Golak babu's assessment that the Pakistani ruling clique would not hand over power to Sheikh Mujib, despite his getting a decisive mandate, was dismissed as 'too much of kite flying' by the 'knowledgeable' folks of Calcutta. My search for an acceptable explanation made me zealously tap every possible source; Professor Sukhomoy Chakravarty, member, Planning Commission and a family friend, Mr Bhupesh Gupta, the CPI member of Rajya Sabha, amongst others. Both came from Dacca and were closely monitoring the developments across the border on behalf of Prime Minister Indira Gandhi. They were her eyes and ears on East Pakistan and, significantly enough, both agreed that denying power to Mujib was a 'distinct possibility'. They were keen to know where I picked up this 'extremely significant clue' as they had heard nothing of this in Delhi's corridors of power, where this denouement was not even considered 'within the realm of possibility'. I was promise bound to Golak babu not to disclose his identity and evaded the issue. I was nowhere near getting a clear pointer and was getting increasingly restless.

I turned to more informed people in Calcutta's journalistic circles, including its two leading lights, Prafulla Ray Chowdhury, Calcutta bureau chief of the *Patriot,* and Chittabrata Roychowdhury, chief reporter of West Bengal CPI's mouthpiece, *Kalantar*. Chittabrata babu suggested that I meet Ramen Mitra, husband of the legendary Tebhaga peasant movement leader of undivided Bengal, Ila Mitra, at their government flat in Entally. Ramen babu, an ex-zamindar, had been an active member of the banned Pakistan Communist Party in the fifties and was a well-known member of the underground communist party. He had built up a vast network of contacts across Pakistan's political spectrum during his underground days. Even after settling down in Calcutta with his wife, he had kept up with his

Pakistani political contacts. Many of them visited him whenever they came to the city.

He confirmed that Zulfiqar Ali Bhutto's Pakistan People's Party (PPP) was more than sure that the Awami League would get a massive majority in the National Assembly on the basis of which Sheikh Mujib would lay claim to forming a government, which would be unacceptable to the leaders of the West. The resultant political deadlock would heighten political heat, tension and tempers on both sides. This, in turn, would result in leaders of both sides indulging in extreme forms of political brinkmanship, which might eventually result in a violent showdown. This, Ramen babu predicted, might give rise to a revolt-like situation in East Pakistan.

This assessment came from Ramen babu's contacts in Khan Abdul Wali Khan's West Pakistan-based National Awami Party, who occasionally communicated with him through couriers. Bhutto and other West Pakistani leaders were busy firming up a set of political options to be offered to Sheikh Mujib to break the future political stalemate, he was told. 'I don't know what those options are but I am sure the Pakistani establishment, especially the military, will not hand over the reins of power to Sheikh Mujib because of their intense hatred for and mistrust towards the Bengalis in general and Mujib in particular.' Ramen babu lucidly explained the post-poll scenario and I waited with bated breath for the elections to take place and for their results. I conveyed Ramen babu's assessment to Golak Majumdar and he said: 'Let us wait and see.'

Yahya's Perfidy

As election results started pouring in, I realized that Ramen babu was a soothsayer. Every word that he had spoken about the emerging post-poll scenario in Pakistan politics was prophetic. Awami League had won 160 of East Pakistan's 162 National Assembly seats and Bhutto's Pakistan People's Party had won 81 of the 138 seats in West Pakistan. The electoral verdict, going by Pakistan's constitutional norms, meant that Mujib's Awami League would form Pakistan's next government by virtue of the popular mandate it had secured.

By then, the Indian Press had begun to take note of the political developments in East Pakistan with page 1 headlines. Even so, Dacca datelined stories with insights into Sheikh Mujib's future strategy were fewer than those emanating from 'Pindi'. Most of them were agency stories quoting excerpts from West Pakistani hardline Urdu dailies like the *Jung* or *Nawa-i-Waqkt*, reflecting the views of the West Pakistani leaders, representing the PPP, the three factions of Muslim League and the Jamat-e-Islam.

All of them were unanimous on one point: Pakistan's destiny would not be safe in the hands of Sheikh Mujib and his Bengali party which they would not trust with the reins of power. Its safety and security and, indeed, its very existence, would be at stake. The dailies reflected the fear of leading West Pakistanis that if the Bengalis came to power, they would return the favour by way of the same treatment of disrespect, discrimination and injustice which East Pakistan and its people had been subjected to since Partition with a vengeance. Mujib's six-point autonomy demand for East Pakistan was labelled as a charter of a secessionist movement. As the main accused in the Agartala Conspiracy Case (Mujib had been charged with sedition for his six-point demand for autonomy), Mujib could not be expected to uphold and fight for Pakistan's Kashmir agenda. More disconcerting for the West Pakistani leaders, mostly from the landed gentry, was Awami League's promise of bringing in legislation to twist the tail of the big West Pakistani landlords if they won, to ensure that they stopped calling the shots in Pakistani society and its politics.

Mujib was anathema to them. The entire spectrum of West Pakistani leaders viewed his coming to power as an existential threat to them, both in societal and political terms. The military and its business class, the generals and the captains of industry like the Adamjees and the Ispahanis, knew that Mujib and his one-time mentor, Maulana Bhasani, thought poorly of the Pakistani state, especially its defence establishment that had left East Pakistan undefended against any possible Indian aggression during the 1965 Indo-Pak war.

General Yahya Khan hoped against hope that Mujib's Awami League would not get the majority and that the military with the help of West Pakistani leaders would be able to manipulate Mujib. Yahya had also hoped that Bhutto's PPP would sweep not only Punjab and Sindh but also win a large number of seats in Balochistan and the North West Frontier Province. This would help Yahya and West Pakistani parties to foist him as some kind of a counter-balance to Mujib and also as a rallying point and a power broker for West Pakistan's cause and for the military too. Bhutto, understandably, went into a tizzy when President Yahya seeing the 'surprising' poll result suddenly commented that Sheikh Mujib was the Prime Minister designate of

Pakistan. Yahya's 'surprising comment' made screaming front-page headlines in Pakistani dailies. Bhutto was revolted at the thought of having to serve as number two in Sheikh Mujib's government.

Yahya's comment came in the wake of Mujib's unequivocal assertion in Dacca that he was legally and morally destined to govern Pakistan as its undisputed leader. The people had spoken. Though Awami League leaders do not admit as much, in October 1972, Tajuddin Ahmed had told me in a tête-à-tête in his official bungalow in Dacca's Ramna area that many thought Mujib had initially been taken in by Yahya's duplicity largely because he had given the general credit for holding a free, fair and credible general election, for the first time in Pakistan's 24-year history.

Unlike Field Marshal Ayub Khan, Yahya had neither tampered with the poll process nor interfered with its outcome in any way. Immediately after the elections, thus, Mujib did not press the general 'very hard' on the immediate transfer of power to him. Tajuddin Ahmed and many others' assessment was that Mujib was probably under the 'mistaken impression' that having held a just and free and fair election, the general was taking his time to attune both the military and the West Pakistani mindset with the processes of restoration of democratic governance to be headed by a Bengali. That would also signal an end to two decades of military rule.

Many disagree with this assessment. Leaders like Kaji Aref Ahmed and Abdur Rezzak of the Bangladesh Liberation Front (BLF) said that Mujib was too far-sighted and knew full well the Pak military's psyche to harbour any such illusory idea about General Yahya. In terms of political strategies, Mujib was far ahead of his contemporaries. They held that he deliberately gave Yahya a long rope to hang himself with. He wanted the military to commit serious blunders, which would culminate in a massive crackdown, resulting in heavy loss of Bengali lives. This would ignite the fire of liberation war in the hearts and minds of the Bengalis to fight back and wrest freedom from the Punjabi rulers. The crackdown would justify the waging of a liberation war by the Bengalis in self-defence. Both said Mujib had so successfully camouflaged his strategy that neither the Pakistani generals nor its politicians saw through his masterfully crafted political game plan.

Thus, nothing politically tangible in terms of transfer of power happened between the announcement of the election result on 8 December and the first week of January. Many construed this to be a crucial loss of time: Mujib could have easily pinned Yahya down by asking him searching questions about why he was hedging around transferring power to him. He should also have questioned the need and urgency for the troops build-up in East Pakistan. In hindsight, and with the advantage of informed analyses that I came across during my posting in Dacca, I found a strong case for such thinking. Mujib initially was willing to give Yahya the benefit of the doubt but took quite sometime to read through his pretentious game of political duplicity and deception.

He realized that the general was buying time for expediting the build-up of troops in East Pakistan. Yahya's plan was far more sinister and nefarious: to teach once and for all the recalcitrant Bengalis the consequences of planning to break up Pakistan. Unlike Kaji Aref and Abdur Rezzak of Bangladesh Liberation Front (BLF) most people, even those close to him within his own party, did not know Mujib's secret game plan, which was to decisively win freedom for his people by gradually mobilizing them for a liberation war and secretly seeking Indian help. For years, he had surreptitiously done enough spadework.

Declassified archival materials in India reveal a letter from Mujib to Jawaharlal Nehru in December 1958, seeking Indian help for 'emancipation of his people'. This account is backed by London-based former Research and Analysis (RAW) operative Sashanka Banerjee. Nehru found the letter too hot to handle at that time and put it on the backburner largely because of his preoccupation with the Sino-Indian border dispute. It was perused by his successor, Lal Bahadur Shastri, who wanted to respond favourably to Mujib's plea. In fact, he had even discussed the plans to raise a Mukti Bahini with his security advisors. But the 1965 Indo-Pak conflict came in the way.

Others in the know of things said that Mujib had received daily briefings about Yahya using Pakistan International Airlines' (PIA) Boeing 707 and 727 passenger flights to move thousands of Pakistani troops in civvies from West to East Pakistan. The PAF's C130 Hercules transport aircraft had also been pressed into service for flying troops to East Pakistan. Mujib knew of PIA flights landing in Dacca late at night, supposedly with civilian passengers. They gave the game away with their large heavy boxes and duffle bags and the fact that they were driven straight from the airport to the adjoining Kurmitola cantonment in big military trucks. This airlift of 'unusual passengers' in Pakistan's own national flag carrier continued right up to April even though India, in the meantime, had stopped Pakistan from 'misusing the Indian air space' by its national airline to beef up its East Pakistan garrison.

Pakistan continued to ferry troops by air through a circuitous route via Colombo where its aircraft landed for refuelling on its way to East Pakistan. The Ceylonese government (it had not yet been renamed Sri Lanka) headed by President Sirimavo Bandarnaike had been cautioned by India that it was becoming a 'willing party' to Yahya's sinister design to suppress by brute military force Mujib's democratic movement. She dismissed it as another 'mean Indian anti-Pakistani ploy'. The other reason was financial. Ceylon was earning handsomely in hard currency as landing charges from a record number of Pakistani aircraft flights landing in Colombo throughout the day and until late into night every day. Since Colombo provided a slender but the only quick lifeline to Islamabad to be in touch with Dacca (sea voyage from Karachi to Chittagong took almost a week), it twisted the Pakistani arm from time to time to earn 'sizable extras'.

The wily General Yahya elicited the right vibes to keep Mujib unsuspecting by first promising to go by the universally accepted constitutional norms of letting the majority party leader to form the government. In an interview to an American news agency, the Associated Press, in late March 1971, he said that he accepted without reservation most of the six-point autonomy demands of Sheikh Mujib as 'fair and just reflection of demands of the exploited Bengali people'. He had even assured that many of those demands would be accommodated in the new Constitution to be drafted by the new National Assembly and the new government. 'East Pakistan must enjoy maximum autonomy, which could be ensured only by providing provisions in the new Constitution that would enable it to wholly control its own affairs, administratively and economically.' I read this interview in the Indian papers and, like many others, started thinking that Yahya was getting ready for a settlement.

No Pakistani general or head of state had ever spoken in such warm, conciliatory and effusive terms. Yahya openly favoured Mujib's autonomy demand for East Pakistan and in unequivocal language. This was significant in the backdrop of the Bengali leader having been charged with sedition in the Agartala Conspiracy Case barely a few years ago. That demand was labelled as 'a charter of secession' by the entire Pakistani establishment and was now being made the 'cornerstone' of Pakistan's proposed new Constitution! Many began to give Yahya the benefit of the doubt and veered around to the view that he was not the devil that he was made out to be.

Both Golak babu and Ramen babu knew better. They dismissed Yahya's friendly overtures as 'too good to be true'. That was a 'clever ruse' to fool Mujib and cleverly defang his secessionist brand of politics, they said. Probably Yahya expected his public stance to make Mujib stop giving rabble-rousing speeches that inflamed the Bengali passion and make him adopt a more conciliatory stand during negotiations on the supposed power transfer talks. To Pakistan watchers what seemed curious was that there was no progress taking place on transfer of powers or for lifting of martial law that was a pre-requisite for restoring a democracy and putting an end to the two-decade martial law in Pakistan.

Ramen babu was prescient. Developments in both the wings of Pakistan started happening thick and fast from the first week of January. Bhutto raised Mujib's hackles by announcing that no government could be formed or Constitution be drafted without his support. He said this on the basis of his secret talks with Yahya and a series of other secret parleys, the first of which was held in Karachi on 28 December, without Mujib's knowledge. This was to come up with a joint and common strategy to checkmate Mujib's constitutional claim to form the government. The most significant meeting took place later, in Bhutto's own *jagir* Larkana in mid-February when Yahya went as a special guest of Bhutto and spent five nights there. A host of military and non-military measures were firmed up to ensure that Mujib was denied the fruits of the popular mandate. Their innate hatred for the Bengali-speaking Pakistani, apart from the general lust for power, thwarted the transfer of power to Mujib.

Sheikh Mujibur Rahman and people of his ilk were considered half Hindus because of their love for the Bengali script and language and the Bengali culture and their rabid antipathy for Urdu and for their surreptitious links with Hindu India. This perception bound parties of all hues and ideology of West Pakistan and the Punjabi-dominated military. Some of them came up with preposterous theories of racial superiority of West Pakistanis, amongst others, the worth of one Punjabi, Pathan or a Sindhi voter was equal to that of four to five Bengalis. Some Pakistani generals like Gul Hassan, chief of staff of the army, were votaries of this theory and wanted Bhutto to be anointed prime minister.

This theory was very similar to the one propounded by Pak generals that one Punjabi or Pathan soldier was equal to eight to 10 Hindu/Sikh soldiers of India. On the basis of this absurdity, they held that if the percentage of votes polled by Bhutto's PPP and all other West Pakistani parties were to be added, they far exceed the votes secured by Awami League. Bhutto argued that his PPP, which had won majority seats from Punjab and Sindh of West Pakistan, had a greater claim to power compared to Mujib's Awami League, which had secured majority votes of the Bengalis only in East Pakistan. The Awami League had not won a single seat in West Pakistan just as PPP had drawn a blank in the East.

Bhutto's insatiable thirst for power to become the head of the government led to outrageous comments like *'Idhar hum, udhar tum'*, openly articulating, for the first time, the division of Pakistan's governance, western wing by Bhutto and eastern by Mujib. None, including Bhutto, had then realized that this would become a reality in less than a year. Bhutto had already begun to vigorously lobby with various influential interest groups of West Pakistan to keep Mujib and his Bengali political outfit far away from power by any means. Mujib was livid when, in early January 1971, he got clear confirmation from his sources in West Pakistan that both Yahya and Bhutto were indulging in secret machinations to deny him and his party governance of an undivided Pakistan.

On 3 January, he held a massive public rally at the Ramna Race Course where he and all the 160 Awami League elected Members of the National Assembly (MNA) expressed their firm resolve in clear and unambiguous terms that no power on earth could stop them from achieving 'emancipation of the Bengalis from the evil clutches of exploitative Punjabis'. There was also a clear message about realizing their goal of transforming East Pakistan into an independent sovereign Bangladesh. He followed this up by secretly forming a government, appointing himself as its president and Tajuddin Ahmed as its prime minister, in the second week of January. This would, over time and some horrendous loss of life, translate into reality his vision of liberating Bangladesh.

Also in early March Mujib arranged a secret meeting between Tajuddin and the Indian deputy high commissioner in Dacca Kailash Chandra Sengupta (popularly known as KC to his colleagues and friends) to find out what would be the role of the Indian Government in providing shelter and material help to his party leaders and supporters, besides the Bengali masses if they were to flee to India in case the Pakistani authorities launched large-scale carnage in East Pakistan. KC said he would be able to provide a definitive answer only after he had consulted Delhi about this. But his promised next meeting with Tajuddin never happened as the Pakistani authorities had put the Indian diplomatic and non-diplomatic staff virtually under house arrest after his return from Delhi. So Mujib and Tajuddin were not in the know of Delhi's response though Indian policy planners had conveyed to KC that India would unwaveringly stand by Mujib and his people in case an emergency-like situation arose in East Pakistan. The KC-Tajuddin meeting finds prominent mention in Tajuddin's war-time secretary Maidul Hossain's book *Mooldhara Ekattor* (1986).

In the meantime reports had reached Yahya that the Bengali nationalist spirit and sentiment were running high with student leaders already publicly hoisting a Bangladesh flag with much fanfare in the heart of Dacca. It had a deep green background with a red sun in the middle. The red sun was emblazoned with a map of Bangladesh in golden yellow representing 'sonar Bangla'. The Bengali people of all sections and society, even girl students and housewives, had taken to the streets backing Mujib's demand for an independent nation for the Bengalis of East Pakistan. They were in fact parading the city streets with real guns and dummy rifles on their shoulders and appealing to the 'valiant Bengalis' to 'take up arms against the Khans of West Pakistan'.

Yahya air-dashed to Dacca to assuage Mujib's ruffled feathers. He convened the first meeting of the National Assembly in Dacca on 3 March without consulting Bhutto. Mujib agreed with the announced schedule and dared to believe that a breakthrough was in sight. Bhutto was peeved. The unilateral decision of Yahya annoyed him so much that he not only decided to boycott the inaugural session but also warned that he would order the breaking of the legs and head of any West Pakistani MNA who dared to attend the first session to be held in the Louis Kahn crafted imposing architectural edifice; the new Parliament building in Dacca's 'second capital'. To rattle the MNAs elected from West Pakistan, Bhutto spread the word around that Mujib had planned to slaughter them inside the Parliament building, which would be turned into a giant slaughterhouse on the inaugural day with blood flowing like river all around. Pressure was mounted on Yahya by Bhutto and also by one of the factions of the Muslim League and the Jamat-e-islam (which had four MNAs in the assembly) to postpone the assembly session. It suited Yahya's delaying tactics strategy to buy time so that he could further reinforce the strength of his forces in the East. On 1 March, Yahya announced a postponement. Mujib was left with no choice but to announce an East Pakistan-wide non-cooperation movement.

Mujib saw this move as the Pakistani establishment's 'great betrayal of the worst kind'. His patience as well as that of the Bengali masses to reach a settlement on power transfer had run out. He was now absolutely convinced that Yahya's negotiations with him were a sham. His call for a nationwide non-cooperation movement meant that the Bengalis would stop paying taxes to the Pakistani government. He ordered the closure of all government offices and commercial establishments and various institutions throughout East Pakistan along with the suspension of all kinds of transport services. The purpose was to demonstrate to the Pakistani rulers that his word was the law in East Pakistan. Except in a dozen cantonments and sub cantonments, the Pakistan government's writ did not run anywhere in Pakistan's eastern province.

Mujib's word had, indeed, become the law. He had already become the arbiter of the destiny of 75 million Bengalis of the province. Overnight, Dacca turned into a city of mass protests and demonstrations. Yahya's and Bhutto's perfidy had made the Bengalis belligerent. Placards and banners demanding independence for the Bengalis of East Pakistan were flaunted in ceaseless protest demonstrations throughout the province, bringing life to a complete standstill. A sea of humanity carrying arousing banners descended on Dacca streets from morning till evening. At the lead was the Bengali intelligentsia as the Bengali pride and nationalism, hitherto somewhat subdued, burst into the open. Demands for autonomy, the six-point programme and even the handover of power to Mujib ceased to be issues as everything snowballed into one roaring demand for an independent Bengali nation, Bangladesh.

The Bengalis were yearning for a Bengali nation. Their voice was clear, unanimous and vociferous. Banned songs of Rabindranath and Dwijendralal Roy, extolling the greatness of everything Bengali, were on every lip. The songs rented the air as freedom from the clutches of 'three Ps – Pakistanis, Paschimas and Punjabis', became the war cry and mantra. The Bengali identity supplanted all traits cultivated over the 24 years of Pakistani rule as the Bangladeshi flag and black flags fluttered from almost all the rooftops. Mujib's historic soul-stirring speech of 7 March at Dacca's Ramna Race Course signalled the beginning of Bangladesh's war of independence. It was a clarion call to his 75 million Bengalis to free themselves from the Pakistani colonial yoke.

That was the crowning glory to the build-up of the struggle for freedom dramatically gathering steam for the last three months. Mujib's speech had stimulated not only strong stirrings of courage and fortitude in the Bengali heart but also provided them with a road map for their liberation struggle and freedom. Two days later, another respected Bengali leader, Maulana Bhasani, bade 'goodbye to Pakistan' at a public meeting in Dacca. He said Pakistanis had burnt their bridges with the Bengalis and there was no way that those could be rebuilt. The biggest and worst blow came from the chief justice of Dacca High Court, Justice Siddiqi, who refused to administer the oath of office to the newly appointed governor of East Pakistan, Lt Gen. Tikka Khan.

The Bengali defiance was being given a voice over various fora like the Dacca station of Radio Pakistan calling itself Radio Dacca and the Bangladeshi flag being hoisted on top of British and Russian missions in Dacca. The most stunning incident was the burning of the Pakistani flag and tearing down of photos of Qaid-e-Azam Jinnah and making bonfires of them in Dacca and in big and small towns of East Pakistan on 23 March, Pakistan Day. These developments were being relayed to us almost daily from across the border and were being regularly reported in the Indian media, especially in Calcutta.

A very interesting thing happened in Calcutta around then. Two persons, who claimed to be freelance photojournalists from Dacca, surfaced at Calcutta Press Club, around 10 March. They were the first to provide us with a snapshot of what was happening in Dacca and elsewhere in their country. They had sneaked through the border with film rolls loaded with photographs of Mujib's historic Ramna Race Course meeting and were looking for the highest bidder to buy their exclusive pictures in the city's media.

The Statesman's news editor, the first one to be tipped off about their presence in the city, showed no interest as the price they were quoting was considered 'too high'. *Ananda Bazar Patrika*, realizing the importance and topicality of the pictures paid a 'princely sum' to grab the rolls. A picture showing Mujib addressing a vast sea of humanity at the Race Course Maidan in a belligerent posture got splashed on the front page of the morning edition of the ABP edition. The paper was a sellout that morning. All the copies vanished within an hour of hitting the news stand. The demand for an ABP copy was such that vendors sold their copies at four times the price.

The published picture in *Ananda Bazar* became the talk of the town. *The Statesman* readers rang up our office in hundreds to find out why their 'favourite paper' had not carried this 'momentous picture'? We had no convincing reply. The ABP picture had so intensely stirred up the Bengali emotion and psyche in this part of Bengal that it became the sole topic of discussion in coffee houses, tea stalls, trams, buses and trains and also in exclusive clubs frequented by the city's rich and famous, from all communities. There was an upsurge of interest in the East Pakistan developments even among the average West Bengali who had not shown any sign of interest in its former half till then.

Meanwhile, Yahya summoned Bhutto to Dacca for holding joint negotiations with Mujib. They were still keeping up the pretense that a negotiated settlement to break the deadlock was on the cards. Bhutto agreed to play footsie but he knew that the top military brass of the army had begun to prepare a blueprint for a massive military operation in East Pakistan in Rawalpindi's GHQ, to 'break the back of Mujib-led secessionist movement'. In early March, Mujib had confirmed reports that Yahya as well as other generals, egged on by Bhutto, had discussed why Pakistan's state power or even that of East Pakistan, could not be handed over to Mujib and his party. That was not acceptable to the non-Bengali Muslims of both wings of Pakistan. If they went ahead with it, it could result in a political implosion. Bhutto came to Dacca on 21 March under heavy military escort. To the Bengalis, he was the villain of the piece, who had come in the way of Mujib becoming the prime minister. His talks with Mujib and Yahya did not yield any result, though they met and spoke to each other for long hours almost every day. In fact, it only made the three harden their stance on the transfer of power.

The more than 400,000 Bihari Muslims of East Pakistan, openly opposed Mujib becoming the prime minister. They feared that, under a Bengali dispensation, they would always get the wrong end of the stick and their Pakistan dream, for which they had forsaken their native Bihar and Uttar Pradesh in India and come over to settle in East Pakistan, would lie shattered. The Bihari community en bloc opposed Mujib's call for independence tooth and nail and openly collaborated with the military in all possible ways, including raising a militia to counter and keep in check the Bengali militancy.

The result was open confrontation between the Bengalis and the Biharis in various towns, with the military openly siding with the Biharis and mercilessly shooting down the Bengalis resulting in huge loss of lives. Not to be cowed down, the Bengalis took on the joint military-Bihari onslaught and struck back on Bihari settlements wherever they could, leading to huge loss of Bihari lives. These mass killings of Biharis also form a sordid chapter in the run up to the crackdown of 25 March as East Pakistan turned into a veritable tinderbox. Tremendous pressure was brought to bear on Yahya to initiate military action against the Bengalis so that Pakistan's natural ally in East Pakistan, the Biharis, could be protected during the most troubled times and also for the sake of Pakistan's territorial integrity.

Well before these disturbing developments started unfolding, the GHQ's blueprint of 'Operation Searchlight' had been worked upon in 'Pindi' and finalized in Dacca. The blueprint provided a broad framework for the operation and the objectives to be achieved. Those were handed over to Dacca's Eastern Command headed by Lt Gen. Khadim Husssain Raza and Lt Gen. Tikka Khan, who were entrusted with the task of working out its minutest details by taking local factors into consideration. With negotiations in a stalemate, both the generals worked overtime to complete the operational plan. Both were raring to go for its immediate implementation.

The operational plan was kept a closely guarded secret, known only to a handful of non-Bengali majors and lieutenant colonels, who were to operationalize the plan at the grassroots level. They had been briefed about it on a 'need-to-know' basis. The Bengali military officers were scrupulously kept out of such briefings. This gave rise to a suspicion among them that a terrible military action against the Bengalis was in the offing to ruthlessly suppress the popular mandate. All this was conveyed to Mujib. He had begun to work out his contingency plan to deal with the impending military action. As a last resort, some half-baked, wishy-washy formula was offered to Mujib by Yahya as an interim arrangement to buy time and maintain peace but Mujib rejected them outright as by now he knew what Yahya was up to.

Yahya too had run out of options and on being assured by both Raza and Tikka that their forces were fully ready for action, he quietly flew out of Dacca for Karachi on the afternoon of 25 March. Before leaving he gave clearance to his Dacca commanders 'to go ahead with their "Operation Searchlight"'. He reminded them of what he had said during his briefing in February last, when the operational plan was first conceptualized: 'At least three million Bengalis must die such a terrible and violent death that the rest of the population would be forced to eat out of our hands.' He did not want to give any time to Mujib to redraw his strategy and wanted his local commanders to start the operation on the midnight of his departure from Dacca.

Bhutto and 'Operation Searchlight'

Significantly, Bhutto did not fly out. He chose to stay behind in his vantage and strategically placed 10th floor corner presidential suite of the Inter-Continental Hotel. From there he could get a panoramic view of the city's skyline and its two main thoroughfares. He wished to witness whether the army was executing its 'Searchlight Plan' as had been conceived. The hotel staff said that he had kept awake the whole of that fateful night; his room lights dimmed as he occasionally went to the window, separating curtains to see the Dacca skyline being lit up by the blazing guns of military tanks, the flares fired by the army to flush out *gaddar*s or traitors, and the speeding light of tracer bullets.

Standing by the window Bhutto pointed at various directions of Dacca's burning skyline, trying to figure out their locations with help from the room service boys who went in to serve him coffee. He beheld the tanks blasting the office of the popular English daily, *The People*, located right opposite the hotel in seconds. The flames leaping skywards like a forked tongue licking Dacca's entire horizon did not disconcert him at all. Bhutto showed no anxiety or remorse as he surveyed the ghastly massacre outside. Perfectly composed, he spoke to the room service boys in excellent cheer. The next morning, he flew out of Dacca in a special flight and on landing in Karachi made that infamous statement on the execution of Operation Searchlight saying, 'Thank God, Pakistan has been saved.'

There was no news on 'Operation Searchlight' and its horrendous execution by the Pak military in the next day's Indian dailies. There was only a small Rawalpindi dateline news item quoting the Pak Military's Inter Services Public Relations (ISPR) press release. It said that the military had launched an intensive search operation to 'flush out troublemakers', who had seriously disturbed peace and tranquility by creating a law-and-order problem in the eastern province. I read the news with scepticism since I knew that the Pak military was baying for Bengali blood. 'Flushing out troublemakers' was the Pak military's euphemism for genocide, I had surmised. My scepticism became stronger when no international news agencies like the Reuters, AP or AFP, had filed Dacca-dateline news dispatches, even though they had fully functioning news bureaus there, which had lately been reinforced by their Hong Kong-based American correspondents.

I rang up Golak babu, Ramen babu, Brojen Das and Chittaranjan Sutar to convey my apprehension about the news blackout. I was told that Dacca's telephone link with the outside world had been cut off as well as its telex and teleprinter links since midnight. Golak babu gave me enough indication that a massive military operation had started immediately after Yahya's dramatic departure from Dacca the previous afternoon. He also told me that all foreign journalists in Dacca had been herded into a special flight and bundled away to Karachi with strict news censorship laws in force. There was no way that any Dacca dateline stories could feature in the morning's paper. Golak Majumdar had no knowledge of Sheikh Mujib's whereabouts and his fate.

Although the Indian media had slowly started taking an interest in the happenings of East Pakistan, it had no clue as how to cover the earth-shaking event. In any event, the Calcutta media was overly preoccupied with the coverage of the daily grisly killings by the Naxalites and West Bengal's fast-changing political scenario. In New Delhi, Mrs Indira Gandhi was waging ceaseless political battles against her adversaries in the Congress and in the Opposition. Events in East Pakistan got overshadowed by the fast-paced developments at home. The other reason was that the political developments in both the wings of Pakistan evoked a negative response in the Calcutta media. However, a large section of Bengalis were now hungry for news and readers kept calling up newspaper offices to inquire what was happening just across the border. Some London dailies like the *Daily Telegraph* had carried eyewitness accounts of its reporter, Simon Dring, about the Pak military unleashing bloodbath, widespread carnage and destruction in Dacca on the night of 25 March. Excerpts of that report were carried by some Indian dailies, whetting the appetite of Indian readers for more such fearless reportage.

An Indian news agency, UNI, had also begun filing from Agartala, its reports quoting accounts of the refugees crossing over to Tripura. It talked about the massacre of professors and students of Dacca University within its premises. UNI was the first to report the large-scale massacre of Hindus in old Dacca's Sankhari Bazar, where Hindus mostly resided. The military had taken with them Biharis to loot Hindu-owned shops and to forcibly occupy them. A few days later the new Bihari owners put up signboards written in bold Urdu proclaiming their ownership.

It was again the UNI that reported the military blasting of the historic Shahid Minar, the Bengali-language martyr memorial, the symbol of Bengali pride, struggle and identity, to smithereens. It was also the first to report the blowing up of the 400-year-old Ramna Kalibari with petrol and gunpowder. Worse, some 100 devotees were mowed down after the temple's chief priest was first bayoneted. The *Voice of America* quoting the Dacca-based US AID official, Dr John E. Rhode, who had visited the Kalibari, had given a ghastly eyewitness account of countless charred bodies of humans and cattle rotting all over the blasted temple compound. The military would not allow the removal of the dead bodies as they wanted to instil fear in the minds of the minorities.

The blowing up and levelling of the Ramna Kalibari had a diplomatic fallout. It strained Pak-Nepalese relations and I reported it in *The Statesman*. According to Nepalese folklore, the temple was founded by the devotees of Goddess Kali who descended from the Himalayas on Dacca around the 14th-15th century. Over the centuries, the Kalibari had become a centre for pilgrimage for the Nepalese, who offered puja and performed sacrifice there. The Pakistan-based Nepalese diplomats, especially those posted in Dacca, visited the temple regularly. Its destruction drove the Nepalese government to lodge a strongly worded protest with the Pakistani generals that the religious sentiment of Nepalese Hindus had been badly hurt by this 'highly despicable act'. This vital piece of information was first conveyed to Calcutta journalists by the Soviet consulate's KGB chief and principal operative, Gurginov. This had caused quite a diplomatic stir.

On the afternoon of 27 March, I met Bhupesh Gupta, the CPI member of Rajya Sabha, a friend of my father's, and Prof. Sukhomoy Chakravarthy at a friend's place in south Calcutta over lunch. The first question they asked me was about the whereabouts of Sheikh Mujib. I had no clue and an agitated Bhupesh Gupta asked sarcastically, 'What are you a reporter for? Working in a paper like *The Statesman*!' He dismissed my explanation that I was a mere cub reporter who was restricted to police and municipal beats the whole day. I could not sleep that night because his comment tormented me. Professionally, I had no idea how to address my inadequacy and that gnawed at my journalistic pride. The next morning, I saw a Bangkok dateline news report, quoting Dacca-returned foreigners, saying that they had seen heaps of badly mutilated dead bodies being carried in a convoy of trucks outside Dacca for mass burial. This stirred me into action. I rang up my chief reporter to ask whether I could go to the Indo-Pak border at Petrapole to interview those who came from across. I was given a resounding 'no' as an answer. I was 'far too junior to handle this kind of assignment'.

My spirit not dampened, I teamed up with a senior office colleague, Chandra Sekhar Sarkar, and decided to go there on our own on our day off; the next day. With just Rs 50 in my pocket and Rs 100 in Chandra Sekhar's, we left for Bongaon by train. We found the border absolutely deserted with no movement on the other side of the Jessore Road. The BSF commandant, K.B. Singh, informed me that not a soul had crossed over to India from Pakistan for the past three days. 'From what we have heard is that the military is still indulging in large-scale killings. So there is little chance of anyone crossing over today. It is pointless for you to wait here and waste time.'

Months later I was to discover why he wanted me to leave the border that day. This was because the sub-divisional officer (SDO) of the neighbouring Meherpur sub-divisional town of East Pakistan, Tawfiq-e-Elahi Chowdhury, a Civil Service of Pakistan (CSP) officer, as well as Captain Hafizuddin of the 1st East Bengal Regiment, stationed with his troops in neighbouring Chowgacha, very close to the border, had established contact with him. They wanted to see him for his 'help of every conceivable nature'. Chowdhury had even come to the Petrapole border incognito and had held a long discussion with Singh inside one of the bungalows of the customs department at the border.

My gut said that I should ignore K.B. Singh's advice. As a reporter, I felt I should hang around and await developments. So I waited by the roadside till dusk. It was during the evening twilight hours that I noticed some movement at the Pakistani border checkpost, at

Benapole. I saw a lone man carrying two briefcases in both hands heading towards the Pakistani checkpost. Pakistani customs and security men whisked him away to the checkpost from where he emerged after about half an hour. As he crossed over to our side our BSF jawans took him to K.B. Singh's office where both remained closeted for about an hour. I realized that he was a European.

His soiled clothes and haggard look were a giveaway about the travails he had undergone to reach the border. K.B. Singh came out and told me that the person was an Italian company executive who had come all the way from Dacca by hitching rides in trucks, auto rickshaws, boats and passenger ferries, private cars and on pillions of motorcycles. The Italian had gone to Dacca to collect dues for his company when the military operation started. He saw the carnage that the military had launched on the midnight of the 25th from his hotel window. He witnessed the blasting of *The People's* office too. On the morning of 26 March, the hotel authorities asked him to check out as no foreigner was allowed to stay in the hotel. The hotel manager helped him by providing a hotel guide who escorted him to the border against a cash payment of $200. K.B. Singh asked me to accompany him to Calcutta and lodge him in a decent hotel in the city.

It was during the train journey that the Italian, Mr Falacetti, narrated what he had seen on the afternoon of 26 March, while leaving a curfew-bound Dacca. To avoid arrest he and his Bengali escort walked through the narrow lanes and bylanes to reach the city's outskirts. He saw smoke still rising from rows of smouldering ruins of burnt-down shanties. The air was thick and filled with the stench of burnt human flesh. Bodies of men, women and children were strewn all over the place. Shanty residents who tried to flee were shot down by the military. Their bodies lay in the middle of the road riddled with bullets in pools of blood. Once outside the city limits, he did not see the presence of the military. On the contrary, he found people at numerous points in large numbers holding meetings and rallies shouting the '*Joy Bangla*' slogan with Mujib's portrait. He and his guide were stopped at several points by agitated people who wanted to know what had happened in Dacca last night.

On hearing the guide's narrative of large-scale killing by the military, the crowd became more belligerent. Some volunteered to reach the two to the ferry ghat on their Honda motorcycles. Both had to bypass Jessore where fighting raged between the Pak military and the Bengali dominated para-military for the last two days. Armed with this eyewitness account I reached my office at 10 pm and entered the reporter's room somewhat sheepishly. I quietly sat down in a corner with a typewriter and started working on my story. Since I had not been assigned to go to Petrapole officially, I was not sure whether my report would get published. So with a lot of trepidation I typed out Falacetti's eyewitness account in just two pages and left it on the table of the chief sub-editor when he was not there. Fortunately, the chief sub happened to be an Anglo-Indian, Bill Noney, who was posted in Dacca as *The Statesman*'s correspondent, until the Indo-Pak conflict broke out in 1965. He had a good understanding of what was happening in East Pakistan. Suddenly I saw him barging into the reporter's room with my report in hand and inquiring: 'Who is this fellow, Manash Ghosh?'

In *The Statesman's* strict hierarchical system, the chief sub did not know the paper's 'junior most cub reporter'. Expecting a reprimand, I got up from my chair and hesitantly introduced myself. He asked me point blank, 'Who in office sent you to Petrapole?' I said, 'No one,' then added in a soft voice: 'I went there on my own.' He kissed both my cheeks and said: 'Son, you have done a good story. You must have more facts. Where are your notes? Dictate the points you have not reported in your story.' It was already midnight and the release of the edition was getting delayed. Noney sat down with the typewriter and furiously typed up the unreported part of Falacetti's eyewitness account. Two-and-a-half more pages were added to my original report and it appeared as an under block on page one in the next morning's *The Statesman*! Because of late filing, my report could get published only in one of the late city editions, just a few hundred copies of which were printed. (Mr N.J. Nanporia, the editor, was unhappy about this and instructed S.B. Chatterjee, news editor, to issue a written note that henceforth all my on-the-spot reports on the Bangladesh war should be carried in all editions.)

I was woken up at six next morning by my chief reporter, Satya Bose, who violently banged the door of my south Calcutta flat. He had been sent by the editor, Mr Nanporia, who rang him up at 5 am, asking him to inform me that I should see the editor in his office chamber at 9 am sharp. The chief reporter did not know why the editor wanted to see me. 'But it must be important. I only hope both of us are not getting sacked. Young man, you have created a problem not only for yourself but for me as well, at this old age. That is the problem of your generation. You are extra clever. Actually you are too clever by half,' he told me, leaving in a huff.

Fearing the worst, I entered the editor's office with a lump in my throat. Seeing me, he got up from his chair and said: 'Oh, you are a youngster. When did you join this paper? And who sent you to the border?' He then asked what news beat I was on. Before I could respond, he said: 'Your story today is very good. I have received congratulatory phone calls for it. I will instruct the chief reporter to assign you exclusively for East Pakistan coverage. There will be an office car at your doorstep every morning at 6 am, to take you to the border of your choice. But do not get too adventurous. Do not cross the border or be foolhardy. Bear this clearly in mind, if anything unfortunate happens to you, your office will not be held responsible. If these terms are acceptable, go ahead.' He shook hands and wished me luck. I had not seen Mr Nanporia prior to this. But I took his advice very seriously. Because before leaving for office I got a call informing me that two freelancers of a Calcutta English daily, Dipak Bandyopadhyay and Surojit Ghosal, who on their own had crossed over to Comilla from the Agartala border for news gathering, had gone missing. Later it was known that the Pak military had laid a trap for them and they walked into it unknowingly. They were first tortured and subsequently brutally done to death as a warning to foreign media men, especially Indians, not to venture into East Pakistan for news coverage. But Mr Nanporia interacting with me came as something like a shock not only to me but also to my colleagues.

And yet I was hardly satisfied with the reportage of the goings on to *The Statesman* readers going by only eyewitness accounts of people crossing the border. I knew the risks involved in going deep inside in person and report from the thick of things, from the battlefront. But Mujib's call to liberate Bangladesh, over a radio broadcast from a makeshift radio transmitter, had a hypnotic effect on me. So did Major Ziaur Rahman's radio broadcast on Sheikh Mujib's behalf. An inner compulsion to stand by the defenceless and persecuted people also firmed up my resolve to cross the border and do on-the-spot reporting and let the world know what kind of untold atrocities the Pakistanis were committing against the Bengalis.

By then, detailed reports had begun trickling in about the virtual bloodbath unleashed by the military in Dacca since the midnight of the 25th. Mujib had been flown off to a West Pakistani jail after being arrested in Dacca. It was in the late afternoon of 28 March at the Petrapole border that Indian reporters saw, for the first time, the open manifestation of a young strapping Bengali civil servant, a CSP Officer, Tawfiq-e-Elahi Chowdhury, SDO of neighbouring

Meherpur, pledging his allegiance to the Bangladesh government. He was responding to Mujib's call to the Bengali civil servants to join the liberation war. Tawfiq looked every inch a freedom fighter. From his hip hung a holstered revolver tied to a brown lanyard strung around his neck. He was the first one to publicly seek all possible Indian help for his embattled country's liberation war on behalf of Bangladesh; the first official face of the Bengali defiance against the Pakistani carnage.

His press conference made headlines in the next morning's Calcutta dailies. All the Indian news agencies and dailies by then had begun filing reports from Agartala that the Bengali military and para-military commanders, along with their men, had revolted and were engaging the Pakistan military in fierce battles in the port city of Chittagong, the cantonment city of Comilla, and also in the ordnance factory town of Joydebpur, near Dacca. In fact, they had liberated parts of those two cities and other neighbouring towns and were trying to hold on to their gains for which they needed arms and ammunition. This is why they had contacted the BSF officers at various border outposts.

It was around this time that I, for the first time, heard of an outstanding East Pakistan Rifles (EPR) officer, Captain Rafiqul Islam, a man of indomitable courage who was making strategic plans and mounting a severe armed resistance and offensive with his men against the Pakistani military in Chittagong. His tales of valour in evicting the Pakistani military from key areas of Chittagong and also mobilizing political and armed support had become a byword in the region. His name and fame had trickled across the border. He had already assumed the halo of a legendary commander and had become a source of inspiration to all the Bengali men in khaki to take to arms.

The slaughter of over 1,000 officers and men of a disarmed battalion of the East Bengal Regiment in Chittagong's Natunpara cantonment on 26 March was one of the ghastliest episodes of the 1971 crackdown, which turned the tide of the liberation war against the Pakistanis. Bulk of those killed were 18-19-year-old young recruits of the East Bengal Regimental centre who were gunned down in their beds when they were sleeping in their barracks in the dead of night. The other mass killing of the Bengali officers of East Bengal Regiment happened in Comilla's Mainamati cantonment where they were herded into a squash court and sprayed with bullets. Many of the officers were doctors and non-combatants. The Bengali teachers of the Army Public School were not spared either. It spurred the Bengalis in the uniformed services to seek revenge for this treachery.

This mass killing was first reported by an enterprising and courageous UNI journalist, S. Handa (brother of Ramesh Handa, former inspector general of police, West Bengal) from Agartala. His chilling account of Chittagong killings hit international headlines, especially in the British Press. The news of all the disarmed Bengali officers and men being gunned down with brush fire while they were asleep and their bodies dumped into specially dug-up ditches, caused widespread shock and indignation. Many of the young recruits who had taken shelter in the neighbouring hills that surrounded their regimental centre were blasted with mortar and tank fire. The Baloch Regiment which carried out this attack was absolutely ruthless. According to Lt Col. Sajjad Zaheer, Bangladesh Army's military historian, the attack was carried out in a planned and meticulous way. The purpose of killing the young recruits was to rule out the possibility of their joining any armed rebellion group to fight against the Pakistanis in future. Piles of bodies were so hurriedly dumped into the ditches that their limbs, heads and torso were seen jutting out.

Yet the news was not received with the seriousness it deserved in India and overseas. Many Indians were sceptical and thought that the report suffered from a credibility gap. Why would the Pakistanis kill their own disarmed regimental brother Bengali officers and men with such barbarity? Some even wrote about it saying that Indian journalists were practising yellow journalism. Without going anywhere and being nowhere on the ground they were sitting pretty in the safety of their offices and were manufacturing baseless stories to demonize the Pak military. Indeed Kingsley Amis, a highly reputed London columnist, said in an interview in early April 1971 that 'half-baked' Indian journalists were 'cooking up cock-and-bull stories like the Chittagong and Comilla killings' sitting at home.

He thundered that these journalists 'neither had the training nor the experience, courage and ability and steadfastness' to cover tumultuous happenings in East Pakistan. They had absolutely no idea of what was happening in that strife-torn region and were purveying 'baseless and motivated reports' to serve the agenda of some vested interests in India. He had targeted Calcutta journalists in particular after the publication of a Calcutta dateline report in a Calcutta daily that a young Dacca girl Roshnara had blasted a Pakistani tank in Dacca by sliding under it with grenades tied to her waist. Many of us in Calcutta tried to find out the veracity of the report but there was no confirmation. Actually, many Bengali journalists of Calcutta were so impressed by Mujib's persona and his 7 March speech that they got carried away by writing reports which they thought, though fictional, helped his cause. Years later, much of Amis's accusations against the Indian media found a loud echo in the magnum opus of an Oxbridge research scholar, Sarmila Bose's supposedly 'extensive' fieldwork-based book *Dead Reckoning: Memories of the 1971 Bangladesh War* (2011). It was only when Anthony Mascarenhas's report titled 'Genocide' appeared in the *Sunday Times* edition of London on 13 June 1971, confirming Handa's report of large-scale massacre of the Bengali officers and men in Chittagong and Comilla cantonments, that the sceptics were somewhat silenced.

There was no apology though, from those Pak apologists for their uninformed criticism of Bangladesh war coverage by the Indian media. Even Mrs Gandhi was heard quoting Mascarenhas's report to highlight Pak barbarities. That S. Handa was the first newsman to break the horrendous news to the outside world, unfortunately, went unlauded and unacknowledged. As perhaps was Capt. Rafiqul Islam's heroic feat. He was the first Bangladeshi commander to rush and contact the commandant of a BSF border detachment (at Ramgarh) on 28 March, while the battle for control of Chittagong was still raging. He wanted replenishment of arms and ammunition for his men and he got those, though not in required quantity.

This set the trend amongst other Bangladeshi commanders to approach the nearest BSF post for the supply of arms and ammunition. It was in response to this growing trend that then chief of army staff, General Sam Manekshaw, sent Brigadier B.C. Pandey from Delhi to Agartala to facilitate the flow of arms and ammunition to the resistance fighters. Surprisingly, Major Ziaur Rahman's name was never heard for any exceptional act of bravery excepting, of course, performing the public act of defiance with a broadcast on Sheikh Mujib's behalf. His name did figure prominently in news dispatches for organizing resistance to the unloading of 10,000 tons of imported Chinese arms and ammunition on 28 March from a Pakistani cargo vessel *MV Swat*, which had just berthed at the Chittagong port after a long voyage from China.

Taking the Plunge

It was around this time that I got confirmed reports that the Pak military was in a state of panic, suddenly pulling out a platoon of the Baloch Regiment posted at Petrapole-Benapole border as fighting between it and the forces loyal to Mujib for the control of Jessore town intensified. The name 'Mukti Bahini' was not yet being used to identify this motley crowd of armed Bengali resistance fighters. They were called members of the Sanjukta Sangram Parishad taking on the Pakistani military. On 30 March, I headed for Satkhira via Basirhat to witness the battle to liberate Jessore town. I was told it would be safer to take the Satkhira route than go via Benapole to reach Jessore. Chandra Sekhar Sarkar and our chief photographer, Sudin Roy, an ex-RAF aerial photographer, volunteered to join me as also my friend Pinaki Chatterjee of the Andaman voyage fame.

We reached the Bhomra border in the afternoon but were dissuaded by the BSF guards from crossing over as the entire Satkhira belt was bristling with *razakar*s (private militia), who had killed some local Awami League activists. I was unrelenting. The BSF men took down our names and addresses and let us go with the warning: 'Don't blame us later in case anything unfortunate happens.' We had to give in writing that we were entering East Pakistan at our own risk. There were some East Pakistan Rifles *subedar*s who met us on the other side. They rejected my plan of going to Jessore outright because of the heavy fighting. They could not take us there till the town was 'fully liberated'. Instead they made us spend the night at Satkhira's Water and Power Development Authority (WAPDA) guesthouse. If Jessore fell, they could arrange for our travel, situation permitting.

We sat on the back carrier of three cycle taxis, locally known as 'helicopters', and reached Satkhira town at sunset. On the way, we saw the Satkhira road had been dug up waist deep at numerous points and innumerable tree trunks with cement-spun pipes placed diagonally across the road as roadblocks. Even before we reached Satkhira, it was agog with the news that three Calcutta journalists would be reaching any moment. Young freedom fighters led by Kamrul Hassan Khan, general secretary, Satkhira Chhatra League, EPR and policemen in uniform received us at the town's entrance with a hug and the warning that, 'This town is full of *razakar*s and Muslim League supporters. Stay at the WAPDA guesthouse tonight and stay indoors. Don't venture out or meet anyone without our knowledge.'

A huge curious crowd had gathered outside the guesthouse when we reached. They were yelling in the local dialect, '*Kolkata hote sangbadik aise aamader muktijuddhor khobor korte*' (journalists have come from Calcutta to cover our liberation war). Kamrul took us to the house of a relative for dinner, as all eateries in Satkhira were closed. We were served home-cooked food especially prepared for us. It was in Satkhira that I first came to know of the terms *Muktijoddha* for the 'liberation fighter' and *Mukti Fauj* for the 'liberation force' being used widely in conversations. Ensuring our safety, there were bamboo-wielding *muktijoddha*s guarding the guesthouse the whole night. We were touched and humbled by this gesture but did not sleep a wink as the *muktijoddha*s blew their whistles loudly to indicate that everything was safe at the guesthouse.

Early next morning, on 31 March, Kamrul brought the good news that 'Jessore town had fallen'. The *Khan Sena*s, a euphemism for Pakistani soldiers, had been pushed back to Jessore cantonment.

Fighting was still on in the town's fringes though, including Peelkhana, the headquarters of the local EPR battalion. The military might have staged a tactical retreat but there was the strong possibility of the Balochis and Pathans of the Baloch Regiment and Frontier Force Regiment charging out of the cantonment with Jessore-based armoured columns to recapture the town. I was told a fire brigade truck would be going to Jessore with replenishment of arms and ammunition and EPR reinforcements. If we wanted to hitch a ride, we could. 'Of course, do so at your own risk.' We did.

None of us batted an eyelid as we hopped on to the truck overflowing with heavily armed EPR reinforcements. The young *muktijoddha*s of the town had crowded around the truck to bid the EPR men and us a goodbye. Around 45 years later I had a chance encounter with Kamrul Hassan Khan at the daily *Janakantha* office in Dhaka, where he was the news editor. In 1971, he was a college student and an active participant in the liberation war. He recognized me at once. He recalled how scared he was about my safety and that of my friends when he bade us goodbye on that eventful day of 31 March.

The EPR signal unit in Satkhira had just received a message that a massive counter attack, including a possible air attack, by the Pakistanis was in the offing. He was afraid that by the time we reached Jessore in the afternoon, the counter attack might have begun in full swing and we might get caught in the crossfire. 'I was praying for that not to happen. Let this not be the last time that I was seeing you all. I once felt like warning you that your Jessore mission was too dangerous. I seriously doubted whether you all would return to Calcutta safe and sound. But my freedom fighter's spirit prevented me from telling you that.'

As the truck wound its way to Jessore through towns like Navaron, Jhikargacha and Sharsha, it was stopped by cheering crowds holding aloft Bangabandhu's portraits and chanting '*Joy Bangla*'. The EPR men were garlanded and treated with green coconut water and sweets. When the crowd found out Calcutta journalists were on board and going to Jessore to cover the *muktijuddho*, there was an outpouring of gratitude towards India. '*Shudhu India-ee aamader sahajya ebong bachate parey. Aamader muktijuddho sambandhey kagojay beshi korey likhun. Kenona aamader pashey keu nei*' (Only India can help us. Write more about our liberation war in your paper. In this war we have none else but India by our side). A young college teacher at Jhikargacha and several of his students got on to the truck to embrace us. '*Aamader durdiney aapnara aamader pashey darate eshechen. Kemon korey aapnader ei reen shodh korbo? Aapnader mehmendari korar shujog pachchi na*' (You have come during our most troubled times. How do we repay our debt? We are not getting any chance to be adequate hosts). I had to cut them short by reminding them that we had come to cover the *muktijuddho* and not to be lavished over with hospitality.

Chachor, on the outskirts of Jessore town, still had a derelict *rajbari* (palace) with a big *jheel* (waterbody) in front. When our truck reached Chachor, it was stopped by the wailing *muktijoddhas* who wanted Sudin Roy and me to get down and accompany them to the *rajbari* to see the genocide perpetrated there by the Pak Army before it was forced to retreat to the cantonment. Dead bodies had been heaped one above the other in a massive pile, resembling a pyramid. The bodies were mostly of women and children and were stacked in the *jheel;* its waters red with the blood of the slain. Many bodies were still oozing blood. Women were mostly clad in burkhas. The people killed in Chachor were the locals, targeted by the military as retribution for the stiff resistance that the *muktijoddhas* had put up there against them.

The scene was so ghastly that Roy refused to take pictures of the Chachor genocide. My senses were benumbed and I was left speechless. Sounds of gun and mortar fire were still reverberating in the air. There were telltale signs of a fierce battle everywhere; bullet-riddled, abandoned Pak military jeeps were burning in the middle of the road; an abandoned three-ton military truck in the middle of the road with bloodied bodies of Pak soldiers. From Chachor, we headed for the Jessore collectorate building where the Bangladeshi flag had been hoisted. I saw youths with bandoleers across their chest and waist and .303 rifles slung from their shoulders marching up and down the roads. They were digging large graves for mass burial of their fallen comrades in arms.

I went round the town for over two hours to talk to a wide cross section of Jessore people in a captured Pak military jeep to gauge the local mood and spirit. The spirit was quite indomitable even though the people had no water, electricity or even food to sustain themselves for the past four days. With little save indomitable courage and firm resolve to take the liberation war to its logical conclusion, they had taken on the Pak Army. I was convinced that it would be well-nigh impossible for Pakistan to deny independence to these bravehearts of its breakaway eastern province.

When our jeep neared the Jessore fire station, the drone of two slow-moving small aircraft engaged the attention of the EPR men accompanying me. They got off the jeep and clambered on to the steps of an under-construction fire brigade watchtower and started firing at random at both the low-flying aircraft. The aircraft had been sent on a recce to locate the positions of *muktijoddha*s in the town. The staccato and crackle of gunfire was so deafening that I ran down the watchtower, my heart in my mouth. From there, I was driven to EPR barracks to see how the EPR men, by strategically positioning themselves, had pinned down the numerically superior Pakistani military in the cantonment area. Not just in numbers, the military had by far superior firepower. The earthen bunker where

I sat came under heavy fire and the EPR fighters there asked me to move out for my own safety because it had crumbled. From the barrack bunker I could clearly see the Pakistani military positions in the distance. The Jessore cantonment's brigade headquarters still had the Pakistani flag flying.

I had found the focus of my Jessore dispatch. It would be the Bengali resistance against the Pakistanis. Instead of wilting and buckling under pressure, the Bengalis were fast garnering mass support and gathering strength and had the stamina to continue their fight. Come what may, they would settle for nothing short of independence under the Bangabandhu's leadership. I realized that Yahya and Bhutto had committed a historic blunder by unleashing the military on the Bengalis and that Pakistan was certainly destined to break up. Around three in the afternoon I decided to leave Jessore. On the way out of the town, our vehicle was stopped by the white cassock-clad Italian fathers and nuns of the Lady Fatima mission. They had trooped out of the seminary on hearing that Indian journalists were heading back to Calcutta.

They handed over a dozen letters to me with the request that they be posted to Italy. 'We are totally out of touch with our church in Rome for almost a month because of snapped communications. We shall be grateful if you kindly pay the postage,' said the head of the mission in broken English. On our way back to the Benapole-Petrapole border I saw, for the first time, streams of panicky and terror-struck refugees, mostly dhoti-clad Hindus, with meagre belongings like pots and pans on their heads, heading towards the Indian border. There were innumerable women with babes in arms and old widows in that procession of destitutes.

My story was splashed on the front page along with a dramatic picture of mass graves being dug in the grounds of the Jessore collectorate. The entire back page of the paper carried pictures of battle-scarred Jessore, its *muktijoddhas* on the battlefront fighting the Pak Army and, of course, the ghastly scenes of the Chachor massacre. There was also a small box story, on the influx of refugees from East Pakistan. That day, my report became Calcutta's talking point and copies of *The Statesman* were sold at a premium. I received a congratulatory phone call from Ajit Bhattacharjea, deputy editor, *The Times of India*, Bombay. He told me that he would include my Jessore report in his book *Dateline Bangladesh* to be published by Jaico soon.

My editor, Nanporia, again called me to his chamber to congratulate me. More importantly, he wanted to know the extent of refugee influx from East Pakistan. I told him that what had started just as a trickle on 27 March might soon assume the proportion of a deluge. He was shocked to learn this and his countenance turned grim instantly. I told him that the Pak military had started targeting the Hindus and these killings would get worse in the next few days, especially in the districts of Faridpur, Jessore, Comilla, Mymensingh, Khulna and Barisal, where there was a Hindu concentration.

Nanporia's immediate reaction was: 'India will be swamped by refugees. We shall get destabilized, economically and politically.' The next comment saw my jaw dropping. 'We should not allow the refugees to cross the border. If need be we must shoot them down.' There was another shock waiting for me. Nanporia said that many editors of other national dailies agreed with his views. I pointed out that 'the border was so porous that no amount of gunning down of refugees along the border could stem their flow as long as a well-planned and ruthlessly executed genocide was on in East Pakistan.' Nanporia's response sent chills down my spine. 'India should have nothing to do with the happenings in East Pakistan. Yesterday, Fakhruddin Ali Ahmed called to say that he had advised Indira Gandhi that the Indian government should stay far away from

Pakistan's internal politics. India should not get itself sucked into a vortex of international chicanery and Pakistan's nasty game of deception and duplicity.'

Whether Pakistan continued with its military rule or refused to hand over power to Mujib was not India's concern. After all, it was not India's responsibility to restore democracy in Pakistan. Fakhruddin had used a Hindi line: '*Humne kya parosi desho mein democracy wapas laane ka theka liya hai kya*?' (Have we taken the contract to restore democracy in India's neighbouring countries?) Nanporia believed that Fakhruddin was right. He also told me that there were other ministers in Indira's cabinet, including the foreign minister, Swaran Singh, who did not entirely approve of Mrs Gandhi's policy on East Pakistan. He shared his views with *The Statesman* editor but preferred to remain quiet for 'discretionary reasons'.

I pointed out that the steady flow of refugees was the result of a deliberate policy of utter thuggery and barbarism being pursued by the Pakistan government to rid its eastern province of all kinds of minorities and secular Muslims. They were being systematically forced to seek refuge in India. The minorities and secular elements had no other option but to escape from religious persecution. Nanporia had no answer. I reasoned with him that India gunning down the terror-stricken, hapless refugees inside our territory would be much worse than what was being done by the Pakistanis. Our image the world over would not only get badly tarnished but we would also be unanimously castigated. Its intensity would be far greater than what was being experienced by Pakistan. Returning to the reporters' room, I realized how true was the belief that leading editors in India lived in ivory towers and had no idea of ground realities.

Amidst the agonizing conversation with my editor, what made me happy were the phone calls from Bhupesh Gupta, Abani Lahiri and Sukhomoy babu from Delhi, who said that my Jessore report had cleared many of their doubts about the fate of the liberation war and its outcome. The report was a first by a foreign correspondent from the 'inside' of the war zone with on-the-spot reporting and photo illustrations at considerable risk to his life. Peter Hazelhurst, the Delhi-based South Asia correspondent of the *Times,* London, read the report and landed in Calcutta the next day to report on Bangladesh. My reports were the talk of the town not only in Calcutta but also in Delhi's South Block, where our policy planners closely pored over them. To my utter surprise, a call came from one Lt Gen. B.N. Sarkar of the army headquarters in Delhi who said that he wanted to meet me during his next visit to Calcutta. My inquiries about him revealed that he was among the top brass of the Indian Army and a 'close buddy' of General Manekshaw who called him by his nickname, 'Jimmy'. When he came to Calcutta in May he had me over at the Fort William's United Services Institute for dinner. That meeting was an education for me because it provided me with an insight into what the Indian establishment was thinking about its role in the Bangladesh imbroglio.

What I could glean from my interaction with him was that he was one of the 'key back-room boys' of Sam Bahadur who had also nominated him as his personal representative to attend key meetings on Bangladesh held in both the North and South Block in Delhi. Manekshaw had picked him for this role since he was a Bengali and was on excellent terms with senior Bengali civil servants like 'Kaalo' Ashoke Mitra, chief economic adviser to the prime minister, and 'Shaada' Asok Mitra, ICS, secretary of a key ministry in the Indian government, both of whom were kept in the loop by Mrs Gandhi while taking decisions on Bangladesh. Manekshaw had also entrusted him with responsibilities like drawing up key strategy papers on Bangladesh for the army. This kept him busy for almost 20 hours a day at his office in army headquarters. His involvement in military matters pertaining to Bangladesh became such an obsession that he did not return to his Krishna Menon Marg bungalow for days together, though he had a seriously ailing wife at home. And when he was assigned to the war room by Manekshaw this became a regular practice which badly pricked his conscience when his wife passed away. Overnight he became an ascetic and spent his life in the service of Ramakrishna Mission Institute of Culture at Golpark.

The Jessore coverage had whetted my appetite for making deeper and more daring forays into erstwhile East Pakistan. From 2 April, I began making daily trips to Gede-Darsana border. Every day I travelled 300 to 400 kms from 6 am until midnight and then returned to office to report. I slept for no more than four hours. I would leave the office car behind at the BSF border post at the Gede railway station, the Indian railhead on the India-East Pakistan border, and walk over a kilometre along the railway track to reach the Darsana station on the other side. The BSF men had warned me not to walk on foot as long suspension of train services between India and Pakistan had resulted in the railway track beyond the Gede station getting covered with wild shrubs, which had turned the stretch into a haven for deadly snakes. There was also a swirling *nullah* that could be crossed only by performing critical balancing acts on the rail track. My first crossing into Darsana was quite perilous and remains vividly etched in my memory. 'Welcome to Bangladesh' was the sign both in English and Bengali, which greeted me as I stepped over from no man's land into Darsana station compound.

A curious crowd had collected to see this person from India coming to Darsana at such a critical time. There was cheering all around when they learnt that I was a Calcutta-based Indian journalist and had come to cover *Bangladesher Muktijuddho*. The station master of Darsana railway station came running to me on learning that I was a reporter from *The Statesman*. I handed over some copies of that day's *The Statesman* to him. That day's paper carried news reports of the growing Bengali resistance in key towns of East Pakistan. He put me on a Mukti Bahini jeep which drove me to Chuadanga, through lush green fields as the connecting road had been dug up at numerous points. Bridges and culverts too had been blown up. Chuadanga, a sub-divisional town, 10 km west of Kushtia, was then the headquarters of the south-western command of Mukti Bahini and a focal point of the Bengali resistance. Headed by an intrepid and strapping young EPR wing commander, Major Abu Osman Chowdhury, and the locally elected Member of the Provincial Assembly (MPA), Dr Ashabul Haq, a staunch follower of M.N. Roy and wedded to Roy's principles of radical humanism, both complemented and supplemented each other's war efforts.

Soon after the crackdown of the 25th, they set up a command council of *muktijoddhas* in Chuadanga to plan and execute military operations against the Pakistanis in Kushtia, Faridpur, Jessore and Khulna districts. In terms of physical size, it was the biggest operation command council initially. On the afternoon of 1 April, I reached the command headquarters located in a district council *dak bungalow*, from where both Major Osman and Dr Ashabul Haq directed their operations. I found a small truck with a posse of men in civvies sitting at the back, armed to their teeth. Suddenly I found Col. A. Chakravarty of the BSF (I forget his designation since he had just been sent on deputation from the army) emerging from inside the building and heading straight for the truck. He signalled me to come but only to tell me 'do not report on my presence here'.

Dr Haq was an impressive and inspiring leader and looked every inch a revolutionary. His highly emotional and rousing speeches, delivered in his stentorian voice, were awe-inspiring. He carried two small pistols with decorated butts, on either side of his hips, tucked inside two neatly crafted leather holsters strapped to his waist belt. A product of Calcutta Medical College, on being told that I was a journalist from Calcutta who had come to cover the *muktijuddho*, his first question was whether I knew his 'bosom friend', Gour Kishore Ghosh. I told him I was too junior to know him and he said he had very pleasant memories of his younger days in Calcutta. To avoid any further embarrassment to Col. Chakravarty, Dr Haq hurriedly ushered me into the operation room where Major Osman was seated at his desk. He saw my office ID card and said without hesitation: 'We desperately need help and Col. Chakravarty had come to arrange that.'

Major Osman was instrumental in launching an attack on a Baloch detachment in Kushtia town on 27 March with the help of a ragtag force of 600 men, which also included civilian volunteers. About 70 Balochs survived the attack and fled in a convoy of trucks and jeeps towards Jessore. But the convoy was booby-trapped and fired upon 25 km south of Kushtia by Major Osman's forces. The survivors tried to flee but were hunted down by the armed Bengali village mobs. Except for one Lt Ataullah Shah, whom the EPR men rescued, none survived. I met him at the Chuadanga sub jail. His face was so badly bruised and swollen because of the battering he got that it was completely out of shape and his head was heavily bandaged. On being told that an Indian journalist had come to see him, he started crying profusely.

The first thing he told me was, 'Back home I have a small darling of a daughter, Nasima. Please report about me in your paper that you had seen me alive in Chuadanga jail. That would provide some consolation to her and my family that I might return home someday. Please, I beg of you to take my picture and publish it along with your report.' I was moved to tears and assured him that his wish would be fulfilled. From behind bars, he stretched out both his hands and said: 'Hold my hand and promise that this soldier's wish will be kept.' Our staff photographer, Shyamadas Basu, who was accompanying me, clicked his camera to record this moving dramatic moment. On my return, I kept my promise by doing a separate story on Lt Ataullah, which was carried with his photograph in the inside page.

While returning to the Chuadanga headquarters, I asked Dr Ashabul Haq a straight question: 'With Mujib in Pakistani prison, who will be the helmsman of your liberation war and from where in Bangladesh will he lead the fight?' I also wondered if he had the resources to wage such a war. 'You need a large pool of unquestionable, committed political leaders and bureaucrats, technocrats and military commanders of proven merit to provide an umbrella for conducting and directing the liberation war and taking it to its logical conclusion,' I pointed out. He took me aside and said: 'It seems you don't know that some of the senior most leaders of Awami League, including Tajuddin Ahmed, Barrister Amirul Islam, A.H.M. Qamruzzaman and Sohrab Hossain have already crossed over to India. Your BSF big guns were at the Kushtia border to receive Tajuddin. I had a hand in ensuring their safe passage through our command area into India.'

Dr Haq was effusive about Tajuddin Ahmed's reputation and standing in the party. In fact, he quoted the Bangabandhu's clear and unambiguous instruction to the Awami League leaders that Tajuddin would lead the liberation struggle in his name, if he were put behind bars. Tajuddin was someone who inspired confidence of one and all for his honesty, integrity, a deep sense of purpose and, above all else, for his organizing ability and academic brilliance. He was the number two in the Awami League hierarchy and a man of letters, and had been the party's general secretary for three consecutive terms. Besides, he enjoyed Mujib's total confidence and was one of his few trusted lieutenants.

To my second question, his answer was quite categorical: 'Of course, our party has a big pool of leaders who can lead our people to victory. But India will certainly have to provide us shelter and help for conducting the *muktijuddho*. Where else do we go or turn to for help? To Burma, Nepal, Bhutan? Or to China? When we eventually get pushed back across the border from our liberated areas by the Pakistanis, we shall have to stay within Indian territory along the border and wage our war of attrition against the Pakistanis with your help.'

On my return to Calcutta, I got in touch with Golak Majumdar and asked him about Tajuddin Ahmed's presence in the city. I shared with him what Dr Haq had told me and found Golak completely silent. He neither confirmed nor denied Tajuddin's coming to India. Suddenly he disconnected the line. A day later, Sukharanjan Sengupta, my senior in *Jugantar*, then a leading Bengali daily of Calcutta, confirmed that both Tajuddin Ahmed and Amirul Islam had been flown off to Delhi, after reaching Calcutta on the midnight of 29 March, to meet Indira Gandhi.

Crossing the Mighty Padma

On my fourth trip to Chuadanga on 7 April, I was surprised to find an anglicized, middle-aged, bearded man, wearing a felt hat and clad in a smart pair of trousers and bush shirt talking in impeccable Oxonian English in a resonant voice to Major Osman, who introduced him to me. His name was Nurul Kader Khan, deputy commissioner, Pabna, a CSP officer, who had come to Chuadanga to collect replenishment of arms and ammunition. He informed me that Pabna was liberated on 29 March by a mixed force of EPR, police and civilian volunteers, who had jointly wiped out a company of the 25th Punjab Regiment, which had already indulged in mass killing and was planning to undertake with reinforcements arriving large-scale slaughter in the district town and its neighbourhood. 'I am going back to Pabna this evening with arms replenishment. We have exhausted all our stocks of ammunition. If Pabna does not get these replenishments, there will be total mayhem.'

He asked me whether I, photographer Shyamadas Basu and my reporter colleague Chandra Sekhar Sarkar, were interested in joining him. He warned us though that it would be a highly risky trip. 'I will be carrying a huge pile of arms, ammunition and dangerous explosives in a special train comprising one engine and two coaches.' However, the train could leave only if an engine driver was found. 'After the crackdown, all the Bihari engine drivers have fled from their railway quarters in Chuadanga. Moreover, the chances of our special train getting derailed are very high because the railway tracks may have been uprooted at many points. If there is a derailment the whole train might explode and turn into an instant inferno. If you still want to join me, you shall be doing so at your own risk. Think it over and decide,' was Nurul Kader's advice.

Major Osman told us that it would be foolhardy to 'go very deep inside' because we did not know the topography, the local dialect and looked different from the locals. 'And, of course, there is this mighty Padma, which will be an insurmountable natural hurdle to your quick escape in case of an emergency.' I said that I would 'never get another chance like this to report a war. This opportunity comes once in a lifetime.' So we reached the Chuadanga station at 5 pm. Big wooden crates containing arms, ammunition and explosives were being loaded into the two rickety coaches with utmost care. Both Nurul Kader and Major Osman repeatedly instructed the engine driver not to go over a speed limit of 10 kms per hour. The train left Chuadanga at 6 pm hoping to reach Iswardih, Pabna's nearest railhead, 70 km north west of Chuadanga around 4 am.

We all sat on two heavy wooden boxes marked 'dangerous explosives'. Armed EPR men sat next to windows with their guns ready to shoot in case of an attack on the train. As the train chugged its way at a snail's pace through all the pervading calm and the descending stillness of the pitch-dark night, I was overpowered by an eerie feeling. Sensing that I was getting tense, Nurul Kader engaged me by telling me stories of how he had thrown open the door of the district police armoury to freedom fighters to arm themselves. He also shared his extremely 'personal thought' of giving up his family title of Khan after seeing the atrocities that the *Khan Sena* had committed 25 March onwards. 'Any Bengali with a Khan title now feels ashamed to mention it. I know of many of my friends who have stopped using their *Khan* title because it has become a pejorative term.'

Throughout the journey, Nurul Kader got radio messages on his portable wireless set informing him about the whereabouts of the nearest Pak military positions. He recalled his Oxford University days and said that he had many Indian Bengali batchmates, both in Oxford and Cambridge, like Ranu Ghosh. When I told him that she had joined the West Bengal cadre of the Indian Administrative Service, he said 'please convey my greetings to her'. Suddenly, our special train came to a halt with a big jolt at the Poradah station. The curious station master had abruptly stopped the train as he wanted to know who was travelling in it and the nature of consignment it was carrying.

He got such a mouthful from Nurul Kader for his *bayadobi* (affrontage) that he asked the engine driver to start his train immediately. When the train reached the Hardinge Bridge it slowed down even more. Eventually it was flagged to a complete stop. The local station master came rushing with a red flag in his hand, telling the engine driver that he was not sure whether the entire stretch of the railway tracks on the bridge was intact. He asked the driver to put on the headlight of the engine so that he could see whether the tracks ahead of him were intact. He advised him to run the train very slowly.

As an extra safety measure the driver asked his fireman to walk in between the tracks ahead of the engine. It took the train almost an hour to cross Hardinge Bridge. My greatest disappointment that night was that I could not see the much talked about mighty Padma's legendary vastness and the ferocity of its waves. We reached Iswardih at 4:30 am to be greeted by a large crowd of '*muktis*' on the platform. They were so overjoyed to see Nurul Kader bringing such a large consignment of arms and ammunition that they started firing shots in the air from their guns. A convoy of Toyota Land Cruisers took Nurul Kader and us to Pabna through a dirt road carved through the paddy fields. I was told that the Pabna Road had been out commissioned by the *muktis* by blowing up all its culverts and bridges. We reached the Pabna town when dawn was just breaking.

Residents of the town could not believe that Indian reporters and a photographer had come to report on their *muktijuddho* all the way from Calcutta. Boga Mia, the Awami League MPA of the town, stopped the convoy in front of his house and forced us to get down and have *naasta* at his place. A large crowd had collected outside eager to see us and kept chanting: 'We want to see our Calcutta guests and want them to speak to us.' The crowd got so restive that Boga Mia had to go out and pacify them by saying, 'They are not tourists. They have come here for a specific purpose; to cover our *Muktijuddho.*' 'But we want to see and salute [*salaam* was the word they used] them,' the crowd roared in one voice. Suddenly two youths came from behind and shouted the crowd down; asking the people to go home.

The crowd listened and dispersed at once. The two introduced themselves as Rafiqul Islam Bakul and Iqbal, Pabna's two leading *muktis*, who had liberated the town on 29 March , along with the local police and the EPR men. The tough battles they had fought against the Pak military for two continuous days had become important milestones in the annals of the liberation war. They took us to the telephone exchange and the main telegraph office, which had been turned into mini-cantonments, from where they had evicted the well-entrenched Pak military after several rounds of fierce fighting. Even after a long gap of a week, stains of blood streams were all over the floor. They took us to the industrial estate flats which served as torture chambers of the Pak military. There also we saw the drainage outlets bearing thick smears of dried blood streams.

They accompanied us to the Pabna collectorate, which was Nurul Kader's office. There I saw a young, boyish-looking girl, with a boy crop, delivering a message to Nurul Kader. She was introduced as the

14-year-old *muktijoddha*, Shirin Bano Mitil. Clad in khaki half pant and shirt, with a gun slung from her shoulder, she said: 'I have joined the war on my own and, of course, with the blessings of my parents.' I learnt she was the daughter of Pabna's much-respected and influential Leftist couple. Her job was to courier important messages of the commanders of the Mukti Bahini. While I was in Kader's chamber, I suddenly heard a very familiar slogan, '*Chiner chairman aamader chairman, Chiner pawth aamader pawth*' (China's chairman is our chairman, China's path is our path) being loudly chanted outside. For a moment I felt I was back in Calcutta.

This was the same chant that I heard from Naxalites in my city almost every day. But before we could rush out, we heard gunshots being fired in the air. Rafiqul Islam and Iqbal suddenly barged into the chamber with their AK-47 rifles. They said that the Naxalites led by Tipu Biswas were raising anti-Mujib and anti-Bangladesh and pro-China slogans. Addressing Kader Khan they said: 'Sir, we want your order to finish these *Mirjafar*s [traitors] here and now.' Nurul Kader very deftly handled the situation saying: 'Why do you want to spoil your image and reputation of being valiant freedom fighters by killing these parasites of China?'

As soon as we stepped out, Rafiqul and Iqbal took up position behind tree trunks, as Naxalites, their faces covered, were menacingly advancing towards us with guns and swords in their hands. Some also had machetes. Just then a miracle happened. Two small low-flying aircraft of the PAF on a recce swooped down upon the collectorate building, where a bloody face off was in the offing, saving the situation. Rafiqul and Iqbal at once trained their guns at both the aircraft and unleashed a volley of fire. The Naxalites, seeing Rafiqul and Iqbal in action, took to their heels. Nurul Kader summoned us to his chamber and informed us that there were pro-Peking (now Beijing) communist parties trying to subvert the war effort of the Bengalis. Those parties decried Mujib as a 'running dog of India' and extolled Bhutto and Yahya as the 'lions of Pakistan and dear friends of China'.

Just when he had finished speaking, a middle-aged man in civvies barged into the chamber to announce that a big Pakistani infantry force with heavy equipment had landed at Nagarbari ghat in five river ferries from Dacca and was desperately trying to head towards Pabna. He introduced himself as Captain K. Nurul Huda. He had especially come to Pabna to carry reinforcements and arms and ammunition to the battlefront. 'I am rushing back to my post to confront the Pakistanis. But I don't know how long we will be able to hold them. We are trying our best to tie them down at the Nagarbari ferry ghat but they have brought tremendous fire power with them.'

Nurul Kader asked his assistants to go round the town telling people who felt insecure to leave. To Rafiqul and Iqbal his advice was 'leave the town immediately'. He turned towards me and said, 'If you don't want to be caught alive, roasted or shot dead like me, join me. I am going to India. I have instructions to go to India. But we shall have to first cross the Padma on row boats.' It was the season of nor'westers. Already there were dark and menacing clouds overhead. Seeing that he told me, 'If the nor'wester comes before we are able to make it to the other side of the Padma, we are finished. The Pak Army will get us.' Nurul Kader and his assistant got into a Toyota Land Cruiser and asked our driver to follow their vehicle. Nurul Kader, his assistant and his security guards had already loaded their Land Cruiser with five big empty suitcases. His vehicle went to three leading banks of the town. They entered the banks and we waited outside.

Their work in the first two banks was swift and fast. The bank staff and his security guards were seen struggling loading the heavily weighing suitcases into Nurul Kader's Land Cruiser. They were taking a lot of time at the third. We had waited for almost 15 minutes. I heard him rebuking the bank staff for not bunching all the currency notes into wads. I got curious and decided to step into the bank. Seeing me Nurul Kader said: 'When we reach India we shall be needing this money to carry on and sustain our struggle. We are under instructions to cross over to India with as much bank money as we can lay our hands on.'

With all the suitcases, bulging with the Pak currency notes, loaded into the Land Cruiser, our convoy headed straight for the Padma's vast expanse of *chawr* (sand banks), which almost resembled a desert, where the *majhi*s (boatmen) lived in small settlements of thatched huts. Seeing our convoy, *majhi*s of the first village came out of their huts and uttered a firm and loud 'no' when Nurul Kader instructed them to row us across the Padma. 'Look at those dark clouds in the distant horizon. Which *majhi* would dare to venture out with his boat when a storm is round the corner? You are free to cut us into pieces or shoot us down [*Aapnara aamader maira felen kaitya felen, aamra aapnader niya jamu na*] and do whatever you like but we are not going to row you across the river.' The response of the *majhi*s of the second village located at a distance of two to three km was identical. Meanwhile, messages were coming on Nurul Kader's portable wireless that the Pakistanis were closing in on Pabna town. All of us got nervous with time fast ticking away. To make matters worse, the wheels of two jeeps got stuck deep into the *chawr*s. All efforts to extricate the vehicles failed and the two jeeps had to be abandoned.

Being in the midst of a battle and concerned about my own survival made me think strategically too. Before we reached the third village, I told Nurul Kader the only solution would be to flip open the cover of one of the suitcases and let the *majhi*s see what was inside and promise them a part of that. He lapped up my suggestion. The strategy worked. All the *majhi*s of the fourth village pointed to the whirlwind of sand being kicked up by the storm all over the vast expanse of the *chawr*. They said in unison, 'Sir, please hurry up and seek Allah's *dua* [blessing] so that we can make it before the storm breaks.' We abandoned the vehicles at the river ghat where six boats were tied to the shore. By the time we got into the small boats and the *majhi*s had started rowing furiously, the colour of the Padma water had started turning pitch black because of the clouds overhead, and the mid-afternoon sky was enveloped in an all-pervasive darkness and a sense of foreboding.

The *majhi*s said it was an ominous sign of an impending violent storm. Even after half an hour of continuous rowing we were unable to see the other bank of the river. Our small boats were getting tossed around by waves and the fear of getting thrown overboard and drowning suddenly overpowered me. I implored the *majhi*s to save me if I fell off the boat. Their instant reply was: 'No expert *majhi* or swimmer can save you when the Padma is furious.' I quietly started saying my prayers. In the distance we could see a heavy downpour and storm lashing the waters of the river that had turned completely black. Providentially, they were yet to hit us. The *majhi*s started rowing more furiously and suddenly one of them shouted that the bank had been spotted.

When we were about 200 metres from the shore, there began a shower of hailstones, the size of golf balls and even cricket balls, almost incessantly. The *majhi*s asked us to cover our heads, kneel down and crouch on the boat's floor. Hailstones rained on our backs, which were badly bruised. Those bruises continued to cause immense pain for a long while. To make matters worse, our staff photographer, Shyamadas Basu, started getting an asthmatic attack. Our backs were pockmarked with blood clots. When we eventually hit the shore, the storm started with full fury. The *majhi*s asked us not to disembark but to remain still in that crouching position to avoid getting seriously hurt. After about half an hour, when the storm subsided, we were told to disembark. It had taken us full 100 minutes to cross the Padma and all my earlier curiosity and disappointment in not experiencing the Padma in its raging form and fury had vanished.

The first thing I did when I stepped ashore was to warmly embrace all the *majhi*s for their heroic feat in rowing us safely across a turbulent Padma. We all knew that we had had a providential escape. The *majhi*s agreed: 'Allah has saved you all from certain death today.' As we trudged through the wet *chawr*, we could clearly hear the sound of gunfire coming from across the other side of the river. Nurul Kader Khan said, 'The Pakis have reached the outskirts of Pabna and a large force is now at the riverbank on the other side and are on our trail. This is the message that I got on my wireless just now. Fortunately, all the boats on the other side of the bank have capsized in the hailstorm. The Almighty has saved us.'

While getting off the boat, I could see a large curious crowd had gathered at a distance trying to figure out who we were. No Bengali in their senses would dare to cross the Padma in a small boat when a storm was raging. On seeing the Pabna DC, they came rushing with help. The small Kushtia village suddenly came to life. Seeing us drenched to the bone, they took us to their huts and brought *lungi*s (cloth covering for legs) and *banian*s (vests) for us to change into. To warm us up they gave us bowls of puffed rice and hot tea. Nurul Kader came to our hut to inform us that early next morning a local village youth would escort us to the Kumarkhali town, 10 km away, on foot from where a vehicle would be provided for us to reach Darsana border. We left the village at four in the morning. The youth was an undergraduate of Kumarkhali college and a *mukti*.

Local villagers stopped us at several places. They were suspicious about four of us making our way through the village tracks so early in the morning. In one village, residents armed with machetes and swords, confronted us, mistaking me to be a Pakistani Punjabi. I was tall, fair and muscular. They told our escort: '*Punjabi palay orey jete dimu na. O halarey marbo*' (A Punjabi is fleeing. We shall not allow him to flee. We want to kill that rascal). The terror-stricken escort came rushing to me asking for my office ID card. He ran back to the agitated crowd, which by now had grown larger. I could hear him trying to convince the crowd that I, indeed, was a Bengali Indian, who had come all the way from Calcutta to write about the *muktijuddho*. It sounded incredible to them that a Bengali *sangbadik* (journalist) had come all the way from Calcutta to this remote region of Kushtia to cover the *muktijuddho*. The providential presence of a young graduate in that hostile crowd saved the day for me. He saw my office ID card and wanted to know why I and two of my colleagues had gone to Pabna. '*Kintu aapnara ekhaney ki korey elen*?' (How did you land up here?) I told him that if he had any doubt about my Indian identity and credential he could get it verified from Nurul Kader, Pabna DC, who was in a house which was half an hour's walk from his village. The very mention of Nurul Kader changed his mood and mindset and cleared all the doubts about my identity.

His persuasion prevailed and he convinced the armed crowd that I was not a fleeing Pakistani Punjabi but a genuine Bengali from Calcutta. Suddenly the mood of the crowd changed. I saw men clambering up giant coconut trees and throwing coconut clumps down on the ground. The machetes they were armed with to kill me were used to slice the tops of coconuts so that we could drink *daaber pani*. I asked the village headman: 'Why are you doing this? A few moments ago you all were planning to slaughter me. Now you are lavishing hospitality on me. I am puzzled.' The headman said apologetically: 'We are unmerciful towards the Punjabis for all they have done to us. We mistook you to be a Punjabi. You, an Indian, are our honoured guest. Please forgive us for the wrong things we have said and done.'

My Pabna reportage, illustrated with pictures of the *muktijoddhas* and the scenes and sites of fierce Pabna battles, dominated the pages of two successive days of *The Statesman* of 10 and 11 April. The focus of my reports was the grit, determination and steely resolve of the Bengalis to free themselves from the Pakistani yoke. The Shirin Bano story with her picture on the front page moved our readers and I kept receiving phone calls throughout the day. Many asked whether there was any possibility of her coming to Calcutta. Some even left their phone numbers and addresses so that I could inform them if and when Shirin came to the city.

Tajuddin Ahmed was so moved by this story that he wanted to meet me. For over an hour that I was with him at his Theatre Road bungalow, he asked me three questions repeatedly. 'How did you find the morale of the people both in the towns and the countryside? Was the resistance to Pak military rule growing and spreading rapidly? And, of course, how was the breakaway component of the Bengalis, both from the military and the EPR, apart from the police, faring in their fight against the Pakis?' All my replies in the most positive of terms made him happy and more confident. That was clear from his changed body language. He said that he knew the parents of Shirin Bano Mitil well as they were important National Awami Party (Muzaffar) leaders. He thanked me for my inputs and said, '*Aapnar katha shunay khub bhalo laglo. Amay aashosto korlen*' (I am very happy to hear about your experience. I feel reassured). I was bowled over by his frankness, humility and total commitment to the liberation war effort.

Encountering a *Gaddar*

Just as there were the patriots; so were there the *gaddar*s or traitors. One of them, whom I unwittingly met, was supplying the Pakistanis with intelligence on *mukti* camps in West Bengal. During one of my return journeys to Calcutta from Chuadanga, I dropped in at a roadside *dhaba* (eatery) in Alamdanga where a large crowd had collected. There I met this man as I was having a meal, a 'filmi-looking' fellow, in flashy clothes, wearing a trendy pair of goggles with a gold chain round his neck. He sat at my table and introduced himself as Zafar Iqbal, a Bengali hero of the Dacca film industry. He told me that he wanted to join the *muktijuddho* and had left the comforts of his lavish Dacca home and was heading for Calcutta. He had no place to stay there and knew nobody in Calcutta. He wanted to know whether he could stay with me for a few days before he made his own arrangements. He claimed that he belonged to a highly cultured family of Dacca and that his sister, Shahnaz Rahmantullah, was a famous ghazal singer. Without any background check, I brought him home. He stayed there for two weeks and borrowed Rs 500 from me to meet his expenses. When I realized that he was not moving out nor showing any interest in joining the *muktijuddho*, I brought this to the notice of Nurul Kader Khan.

Suddenly, one morning, Zafar Iqbal asked for another Rs 500. He wanted to buy an air ticket for Agartala from where he would cross over to Akhaura and proceed to Dacca. He claimed he was homesick and 'miserable' without his sweetheart, a noted Dacca actress named Babita. He carried her snapshots in his wallet. He showed me her snaps once and said he could not live without seeing her. So he had to go back home. Shocked, I asked, at a time when other Bengali actors from Dacca like Subhash Dutta and Kabori were in Calcutta and handsomely contributing to the liberation war effort, why was he running away to be in the safe confines of his Dacca home and stay close to his sweetheart? This enraged him so much that he instantly left my flat in a huff with his briefcase in hand.

Two days later, Rafiqul Islam Bakul, the freedom fighter from Pabna, suddenly turned up at my home to find out where Zafar Iqbal was. He had been instructed by Mukti Bahini headquarters to bring him to its nearest camp 'dead or alive'. Zafar, according to him, had been sent by the Pak military to collect vital intelligence on Mukti Bahini camps. His sister, Shahnaz, Bakul claimed, too was on the payroll of the Pak military. The Mukti Bahini headquarters had issued orders for his immediate arrest and trial. When I told him that Zafar had suddenly left two days ago, Bakul looked crestfallen. 'Then we shall get him in Dacca.'

In early April, Calcutta had already become home to the first, second and third rung of Awami League leaders and their followers. Senior Bengali bureaucrats and technocrats, besides senior Bengali military officers, including Colonel (Retd) M.A.G. Osmani, had also started arriving in the city in large numbers. Suddenly, they turned Calcutta into a busy hub of those leading the *muktis*. There were so many of them that finding suitable accommodation for them in the city was a challenge for both the central and the state governments. The most worrying development was the ceaseless flow of refugees from across the border. What had started as a trickle on 27 March was fast assuming gargantuan proportions, especially in Tripura and West Bengal. India, especially its bordering states, were not prepared for it.

Meanwhile, Calcutta had been linked to Chuadanga telephonically. Tajuddin and Amirul had already spoken to Chuadanga's western command headquarters over telephone about the progress of the liberation war under its command. The outcome of Tajuddin's meeting with the Indian prime minister in Delhi on 3 April was equally positive. It clearly indicated that the Indian government would stand by the persecuted and defenceless Bengalis of Bangladesh during their most trying times and need. She even went to the extent of assuring Tajuddin that India would not hesitate to become an equal partner in Bangladesh's war of liberation.

This meeting with Tajuddin was, however, preceded by a hitch as Mrs Gandhi wanted to be absolutely sure that, in Mujib's absence, she was interacting with his chosen successor who would be leading the liberation war for the Bengalis in his name. The hitch arose largely because of 'some miscommunication and misunderstanding' caused on the night of 25 March at Sheikh Mujib's Dhanmondi residence where senior Awami League leaders, including Tajuddin, were present. Mujib took everyone by surprise when he suddenly changed his mind and plan and announced that, in view of the impending military crackdown, he would not go underground to lead and carry on the war of liberation.

Mujib feared that if he went underground, the Pak military would run amuck causing such widespread mayhem and destruction that could eventually compromise the goal of the liberation war itself. '*Pakistani ra Lanka kando ghatabe*' (Just as Lanka was burnt down in the *Ramayana* in search of Sita, the Pak Army would burn down Bangladesh if they did not get him). So he decided to stay at home and court arrest. He explained to his people that the consequence of the Pak Army not finding him at his home would result in a *Lanka kando* in Bangladesh, which he wanted to avoid at any cost.

His instructions to his lieutenants, including Tajuddin at that meeting, were: 'All of you go underground in Dacca's neighbourhood and resurface and regroup after the worst phase of crackdown is over.' According to another version he had asked his leaders to go over to India ('*Tora sob India choley ja*'). He gave them a small chit on which was a handwritten Calcutta address – 43, Rajendra Road, Northern Park, Bhowanipore – which he wanted everyone to memorize. He then took back the chit and tore it into shreds. By that Mujib meant they should all go to that address where Chittaranjan Sutar, under his instruction, was already billeted. He did not amplify his statement because earlier in mid-January he had announced the formation of a secret Bangladesh government, at a secret meeting with his party seniors, including Tajuddin, which in his absence would provide the leadership in conducting the liberation war.

In fact Mujib had empowered Sutar, who was his long-time jail mate and in whom he had confided his dream of freeing the Bengalis from the Pakistani shackle, to liaise from Calcutta with the Government of India in his absence. Sutar knew who all were authorized to interlocute with Delhi on behalf of Bangladesh for seeking Indian help. Mujib had mentioned Sutar's Calcutta address to his senior party colleagues in confidence. Should they be forced to flee to India, they should reach out to Sutar, his pointsman in India. Also, in early 1970, Mujib was instrumental in sending his former jail mate, Troilakhya 'Maharaj', an ailing legendary revolutionary of British India days, to Delhi ostensibly for medical treatment.

The real purpose was to open an official line of communication with Prime Minister Indira Gandhi through him and also to apprise her of the evolving political situation in East Pakistan. Both houses of the Indian Parliament, under Mrs Gandhi's leadership, jointly felicitated the Maharaj for his unique contribution to India's freedom struggle, which was a signal to Mujib that the Maharaj had successfully accomplished his assigned Indian mission. To revert to the hitch, according to one version, on reaching Asom Bhavan on 29 March, Tajuddin erroneously asked Golak Majumdar about 43, Rajendra Prasad Road, instead of 43, Rajendra Road, which was the critical location, leading to a confusion.

Tajuddin did not know that Rajendra Prasad Road, which was in the Clive Row area of Dalhousie Square, was not the same as Rajendra Road, which was in south Calcutta's Bhowanipore area. Since there was no house number 43 in Rajendra Prasad Road, Golak Majumdar told Tajuddin that no such address existed. As a result, Tajuddin could not speak to Sutar. Without Sutar's knowledge and nod, he took off on a special flight for Delhi, accompanied by Rustamji, to meet Mrs Gandhi. According to one version, Golak Majumdar had realized about Tajuddin's mix up and should have pointed this out to him. Apparently, there was turf war between the two Indian security agencies and their inter-service rivalry came in the way.

On the one hand, Chitta Sutar was being guarded day and night by the sleuths of the Research and Analysis Wing (RAW). They were directly reporting to the Cabinet Secretariat and the key functionaries at the Prime Minister's Office (PMO). On the other, there was Golak's thoroughly overhauled intelligence wing of the BSF, which had done an exemplary work of not only tracking but also ensuring Tajuddin and his companion's safe passage from Dacca to India's border and subsequently to Calcutta. The BSF's intelligence wing successfully kept both the PMO and Rustamji posted about every detail of these two leaders' journey towards the Indian border.

It was Golak Majumdar's feedback to the PMO that resulted in Mrs Gandhi sending Mr Rustamji post-haste to Calcutta by a special flight. He was to escort them to Delhi for a meeting with her. Naturally, the BSF did not want to let Tajuddin go from their charge and control. The other reason for Golak babu not being able to do course correction between the night of 29 March and the early morning of 30 March, was that he hardly got any time and chance to explain and clear the mix up to Tajuddin as the PMO and various Indian agencies were breathing down his neck about Tajuddin's forthcoming trip to Delhi. The hitch stemmed from Delhi not getting the nod from Chittaranjan Sutar that Tajuddin was, indeed, Mujib's chosen interlocutor.

Within a few hours of Golak Majumdar extending the invitation to Tajuddin and Barrister Amirul Islam at the BSF's Nadia border after welcoming them to India on behalf of Prime Minister Indira Gandhi, a bond of mutual trust, faith, respect and understanding had developed between the three. This laid the foundation of an excellent rapport, which cemented the personal chemistry between them. Golak's thoughtful gesture of bringing Bengali savouries for them was not lost on the fatigued couple. It was to be a long drive to Calcutta in his flag car and Golak was mindful that both would be famished. They had neither the time nor opportunity to have a decent meal during their long uninterrupted march to the Indian border. The chance discovery en route that Tajuddin and Golak for some time were batch mates in St Paul's College, Calcutta (a fact disputed by members of Tajuddin's family), deepened their bonds especially given the unexpected reunion under strange, dramatic and trying circumstances.

Unheralded Heroes

The two Awami League leaders, Tajuddin Ahmed and Barrister Amirul Islam, had taken an incalculable risk in undertaking a long march to the Indian border. The Pakistan military had launched a massive search and combing operation in a curfew-bound Dacca to round up top Awami League leaders, following the crackdown of 25 March. The future of their revolution lay in their successfully accomplishing this risk-fraught and dramatic journey to India and eventually meeting the Indian prime minister. It was, therefore, historic and not just because they escaped from Dacca, from under the noses of the Paki Army, in the guise of poor peasants, attired in torn *lungi*s and *panjabi*s (loose top shirt). Thus disguised, they ventured on their long march through five districts to reach the Indian border. The import of the risks that they took and their grit and determination is yet to be fully grasped by the past and the present-day Bangladeshi historians.

The journey was marked with guile, bravado and presence of mind and left no one in any doubt about their steadfast commitment to Mujib and Bangladesh's cause. This legendary journey was a critical milestone in Bangladesh's liberation war, as were the actions of the two after the military crackdown. Both Tajuddin Ahmed and Barrister Amirul Islam, on Mujib's instruction, went underground in Dacca's upmarket neighbourhood of Lalmatia for two days. Barrister Amirul had managed to call Dr Ashabul Haq, just before the phone lines were cut, and communicate to him their plans to head towards the Indian border via Chuadanga. He was told to keep the Indian authorities posted about their planned long march. Golak Majumdar, who was closely monitoring the day-to-day developments in Bangladesh, at once informed Rustamji and the PMO about this. Hence, Indira Gandhi dispatched Rustamji to Calcutta to receive and escort the two leaders to Delhi for an urgent meeting with her.

There are two versions of Tajuddin Ahmed and Barrister Amirul Islam's crossing over to India. According to Tajuddin Ahmed and his family, the two leaders reached the Kushtia-West Bengal border, close to Meherpur and sent its SDO Tawfiq-e-Elahi Chowdhury and the sub-divisional police officer of Jhenidah, Mabubuddin Ahmed, as their emissaries, to the nearest BSF border outpost with the message that two senior ministers of the Bangladesh government were waiting in a bushy no man's land at the border. Both would enter India provided Prime Minister Indira Gandhi agreed to meet them and only if they were welcomed with adequate protocol reserved for ministers.

As both leaders cooled their heels under the shade of a culvert for almost two hours, they were tormented by questions about how would they conduct the war if India refused to help and what course the liberation war would take in the days ahead. After an agonizing wait they suddenly heard stomping of heavy boots and found a small BSF contingent had arrived to give them guard of honour and escort them to the BSF border post. There they were informed that Golak Majumdar, head of BSF's Eastern Frontier, would be reaching the BOP any moment. Golak 'welcomed' both the leaders to India 'on behalf of Mrs Gandhi'.

There is also a dramatic story around Tajuddin and Barrister Amirul's arrival in Calcutta, accompanied by Golak and the director general of BSF, K.F. Rustamji. According to Golak Majumdar's unfinished memoirs, to which his daughter Jayanti Ghosh has kindly provided me access, the intelligence wing of the BSF had informed him that, after the crackdown, two senior Awami League leaders had left Dacca for the Kushtia-West Bengal border in the guise of poor peasants. Acting on his instinct, on 30 March, Golak reached the Banpur-Gede border and headed straight for the sub-divisional officer (SDO) of Meherpur, Tawfiq-e-Elahi Chowdhury's office. He asked Tawfiq about the presence of the two senior Awami League leaders. Initially, Tawfiq pleaded ignorance but, pressed hard, he presented the two tired, famished and thoroughly dishevelled men, clad in soiled clothes before Golak.

They introduced themselves to Golak, who at once 'invited' both as the prime minister's 'official guests to India'. He also assured both that their meeting with the prime minister was being arranged in Delhi. Golak had both the leaders in his flag car driving back to Calcutta. The BSF motorcade stopped briefly at Dum Dum airport where they met the BSF director general, K.F. Rustamji, who had just arrived from Delhi by a special aircraft. He was keen to meet both the Bangladeshi leaders and asked his intelligence chief, Rajagopal, to talk to both so as to be absolutely sanguine about their identity. When Rajagopal confirmed that both were indeed who they were claiming to be, the motorcade proceeded towards Calcutta.

Golak Majumdar had decided to put up Tajuddin and Barrister Amirul temporarily at Asom Bhavan in Russel Street. He had the state government guesthouse vacated and deployed BSF commandos to guard it. February-March in 1971 was a time when Naxalite killings in Calcutta and its suburbs had reached a peak. The Naxalites had so terrorized the city that its life would come to a halt early in the evening. All the shops, bars, eateries, including fashionable restaurants and clubs, would down their shutters by 8 pm. When Tajuddin and Amirul reached Asom Bhavan, it was past 10 pm and the Asom Bhavan kitchen had closed for the night and its staff had left for the day. There was no cooked food for his VVIP guests; the neighbouring restaurants in Park Street were closed too and Golak Majumdar was in a fix. He had to arrange food for his high-profile guests. His director general, K.F. Rustamji, was just as embarrassed. What if the Bangladeshi VVIP guests had to go to bed on empty stomachs? Having served in challenging assignments, this veteran policeman of 35 years standing, belonging to the IP cadre, always carried an emergency kit with him whether at home or abroad. The kit pack included a mini stove and some cooking oil, so that in case of being suddenly held up in some remote place he could quickly prepare a decent snack for himself. On that night he, as a face-saving strategy, had eggs ordered to his room which he beat up and served as omelette to the two leaders before they had their dinner.

Meanwhile, Golak had turned to his close friend Nihar Chakravarty for help. Nihar babu, a Bengali businessman, was well known in the city's social and political circles for being a generous host and holding lavish parties and get-togethers at his Little Russel Street flat. He had resident *baburchi*s (chefs) who quickly prepared special *shami kebab*s and *pawrota* (parathas). The piping hot food was served to all the guests well past midnight. Tajuddin and Barrister Amirul helped themselves to the food liberally. They had not eaten a proper, home-cooked meal after they had left their respective Dacca residences on the night of the 25th. Golak Majumdar admitted: 'Nihar saved me and India from a big embarrassment that night.'

There was another problem that had to be solved after the two leaders had their dinner. Tajuddin did not have proper clothes for his meeting with the prime minister. Both Rustamji and Golak were ready to share their clothes but those fitted neither Tajuddin nor Amirul. Again Nihar babu came to the rescue and sent a set of his own clothes, which seemed to be a perfect fit. Early next morning, the two Awami League leaders flew with Rustamji to Delhi in a special aircraft. As a precautionary measure, all flight operations at the Delhi airport had been temporarily suspended from morning till the afternoon, so that the special aircraft from Calcutta could land at Palam without any hitch.

However, the flight's delayed departure from Calcutta led to an hour's delay in landing at Palam. The Palam ATC was flooded with endless queries from the PMO about the safety and security of the flight. Once in Delhi, both had to sit for major debriefing sessions, attended by PMO officials including P.N. Haksar, principal private secretary to the prime minister, foreign secretary, the home secretary and senior officers at the army headquarters, as Delhi's policy makers were not au fait with the developments following 25 March, especially about the scale and impact of the crackdown.

Before Tajuddin attended those sessions, he had no idea about the whereabouts and well-being of his senior party colleagues; so there was no scope for holding any discussion with his party colleagues about the strategy to be adopted by him during his first meeting with the Indian prime minister. But it must be said to his credit that his indomitable nationalist spirit and instinct made him say the right things that were needed to be told to Mrs Gandhi for getting Indian support. He had done his homework too. He had correctly read and gauged the Indian public mood and also that of the country's principal opposition parties. Their leaders had, at a special meeting convened by the prime minister a few days earlier, urged Mrs Gandhi not to remain a mute spectator to the grisly happenings in East Pakistan. In fact, the Sarvodaya leader, Jayaprakash Narayan, had even gone to the extent of demanding Indian military intervention in East Pakistan. His trusted lieutenant, Karpoori Thakur, then Bihar chief minister and a die-hard socialist, had issued orders to his police department to throw open Bihar's police armoury for supplying arms and ammunition to the Mukti Bahini. He used north Bihar's Purnea-Kishenganj corridor for ferrying arms and ammunition to freedom fighters in northern Bangladesh. Former cabinet minister Dr Triguna Sen's open letter to Indira Gandhi, demanding a firm commitment of her government to stand by the oppressed people of Bangladesh, emboldened Tajuddin to be candid and brutally frank about what exactly he wanted from Mrs Gandhi at his first meeting with her on 3 April.

What had also made Tajuddin's job considerably easy was the presence in Delhi around the same time of Bangladesh's two leading and most respected economists and academics, Dr Rehman Sobhan and Dr Anisur Rehman, and also the leaders of the Bangladesh Liberation Front. They had sensitized the Indian government about the happenings in East Pakistan post 25 March. Tajuddin was wholly corroborating what Mrs Gandhi had already heard at some length earlier from her advisers.

To return to the unfortunate hitch that preceded his meeting with Mrs Gandhi, it caused a lot of bad blood in Bangladesh politics and confusion in the rank and file of *mukti*s during the liberation war. This issue was thoroughly exploited by Tajuddin's detractors in the Awami League, who not only wanted to corner and run him down in the party but also openly questioned whether he had the qualities to lead the liberation war from the front. They even desperately tried to subvert his installation as the prime minister of the government in exile. At a meeting of senior Awami League leaders in Calcutta after Tajuddin's return from Delhi, Mujib's nephew, Sheikh Fazlul Haq Moni, preferred the formation of a revolutionary council and not a government in exile with Tajuddin as its prime minister. He and some others said that Tajuddin should not have rushed to Delhi for his meeting with the Indian prime minister without the knowledge and approval of other senior leaders of the Awami League. This encouraged Khondokar Mushtaq to throw his hat in the ring in the prime ministerial race. He was persuaded to withdraw but only on the condition that he would be made the foreign minister in the government in exile.

After liberation, these detractors even used this as a ploy to poison Mujib's ears and portray Tajuddin as 'highly selfish and ambitious, one who had become too big for his boots; for this his wings had to be clipped'. To get closer to Mujib and earn his confidence as loyalists, they played games of deception. I was witness to some of them during my posting in Dacca. Unfortunately, Mujib was taken in by this argument and distanced himself gradually from Tajuddin and followed their mischievous advice for which he later paid a very heavy price; his own life. For the time being, of course, Tajuddin was the hero. Once Chittaranjan Sutar confirmed to the PMO that Tajuddin was, indeed, the senior-most member of the secret government that Mujib had formed for leading the liberation war in his absence and that he not only enjoyed Mujib's total confidence but also that of the entire party, the hitch was resolved.

The Indira-Taj Meeting

The Indira-Tajuddin meeting was truly historic. Both leaders struck very cordial notes, never giving the impression that they were total strangers as they candidly shared their views. Mrs Gandhi treated Tajuddin with exceptional honour and respect. Much later, after liberation, Tajuddin had admitted to me in an informal chat in his official bungalow in Dacca that he had not expected the Indian prime minister to be 'so positively open, friendly, forthright and forthcoming at the very first meeting'. He had expected her to be 'circumspect, prevaricating and probing' while interacting with him. He was pleasantly surprised to find her on the same wavelength as he was. What Mrs Gandhi liked about Tajuddin, as Mr Haksar told me later, was his brief preface to his long submission that he had come to meet her as the head of a government of an independent sovereign country, Bangladesh. Accordingly, he expected to be treated with due respect and as an equal. Mrs Gandhi at once put him at ease. That would not be an issue with her and her government, she assured him. Tajuddin's bold presentation went viral both in the Awami League as well as inside Indian official circles many of whom likened his language to that of King Porus who had told Alexander the Great that he wished to be treated by him as one king would treat another. This forthrightness impressed Mrs Gandhi and all those present at that historic 3 April meeting.

At the outset Tajuddin said that he had come to her not to beg but to seek help and cooperaton of her government for his country's liberation war effort. He informed Mrs Gandhi that a government had already been formed with Sheikh Mujib as its president as soon as the crackdown started on 25 March midnight and that he was very much a part of it. Other senior leaders of the Awami League were its ministers. He said that considering the ever-growing scale of the liberation war and popular participation in it, India should allow unrestricted entry of freedom fighters inside its territory for refuge and training and allow its territory to be used by the Bangladeshi political elements for carrying out their political activities without any hindrance. Mrs Gandhi agreed to both without batting an eyelid. Her twin decisions of opening India's border to help Bangladeshi people to carry on their fight were fraught with far-reaching consequences. Her decisions channelized the course of the liberation war on a positive line. It was Tajuddin's sincere, spirited and cogent presentation of Bangladesh's needs for its fight for independence and his vision for strategizing the liberation war that convinced Mrs Gandhi and her advisers that he and his government deserved India's full support as they meant business.

Tajuddin narrated to Mrs Gandhi his personal interaction with the officers and men of the East Bengal Regiment (EBR) and EPR at the Kushtia-India border where they implored him to secure supplies of automatic weapons from India, so that they could take on the Pak Army. Tajuddin praised the unflinching loyalty of those men to the cause of Bangladesh and said that despite being heavily outnumbered and outgunned by the Pak military, they had fought valiantly against the Pak military's Jessore brigade. He did not want to let them down and for this he needed India's help. At that meeting he also made it clear that his freedom fighters would have the sole prerogative of carrying out military operations against the Pakistani forces inside

Bangladesh led by their own commanders and not by the Indian military whose role would be restricted only to training the freedom fighters and arming them.

What perked up that meeting was his narration of the prevailing Bengali mood in Bangladesh. He told Mrs Gandhi that General Yahya and his advisers had hoped that the Bengalis would be shocked into submission after the bloodbath of 25 March; that they would just meekly raise their hands and surrender abjectly. Yahya and his generals were sure that fearing further retribution they would eventually capitulate and give up their fight for independence. To their chagrin and dismay, the Bengalis were quick to overcome the initial shock and came back into the fight with a greater resolve, gusto, commitment and resilience.

The feedback that he was getting from inside was that Pakistanis were taken aback by the growing and the resolute nature of the Bengali resistance. Almost the whole Bengali population had turned hostile towards the Pakistanis and their henchmen. Even in the villages, their residents were providing food and shelter to the freedom fighters. This dramatic transformation of the Bengali psyche in the countryside in such a short time was the transformational force. The complete alienation of the Bengali from the ruling powers was cemented by the genocide of the Bengalis by the Pakistan military that was still ruthlessly trying to suppress the Bengali freedom struggle.

For almost half an hour Mrs Gandhi intently listened to Tajuddin's exposition. She then asked whether the formation of a government in exile at the earliest was uppermost in his mind. That, to her mind, was the need of the hour and it would be through this government that everything that Bangladesh needed for waging the liberation war could be channelized by India. This government, composed of elected MNAs, would provide the stamp of legitimacy to the freedom movement. This legitimacy was badly needed both at the national and international levels. Such a government would also work as a sheet anchor of the freedom movement. Moreover, waging an all-out war of liberation was a herculean task, which had to be conducted by a legitimate government on various fronts. Without putting such a government in place, the goal of achieving a Bengali nation could not be reached.

Before Mrs Gandhi could finish, Tajuddin intervened saying that as earlier stated by him a Bangladesh government was already in existence. Mrs Gandhi argued that not much was known about this government as that had, according to her knowledge, never figured in the public domain and discourse prominently. What was needed was a public government in exile, which should be his first priority. To gain international credibility and acceptability, this government should be sworn in under the full glare of the international media and in an area that was still under the control of freedom fighters. Before Mrs Gandhi could finish, Tajuddin interjected saying he was on the same page as her and was about to broach this subject but was hesitant to mention it because the formation of such a government meant India had to provide the massive back up and wherewithal without which it would not be able to get off the ground.

For Tajuddin two major and most worrisome obstacles were overcome with his positive first meeting with Mrs Gandhi. It was so productive that it removed many of his doubts and worries about how to carry forward the liberation war. Mrs Gandhi's suggestions convinced him that she was serious in what she was saying and meant business. He grew in confidence that a collective and well-coordinated effort of his government in exile and the Indian government would eventually emerge victorious. In his presence, Mrs Gandhi directed the officials present, especially Rustamji, to extend all the help that Tajuddin Ahmed and his government would require from time to time.

The Indian assessment of Tajuddin Ahmed, as told to me by Mr Haksar much later, was that it was only he who, in Mujib's absence, was mentally and intellectually endowed to lead the Awami League and assimilate the support of various disparate political groups and parties for the liberation war. His plans and programmes for waging the liberation war were unique in their conception and formulation and were in line with those of the Indian government. His unwavering commitment to Mujib and the Bangladesh cause made him stand out as the tallest among a host of other Awami League leaders whose sole obsession was that the Indian Government should grant immediate diplomatic recognition to the Calcutta-based Bangladesh government and order the military to intervene to achieve freedom for the Bengalis. They envisioned a free and independent Bangladesh achieved primarily through India's military and diplomatic moves.

But Tajuddin stood apart from this crowd of leaders jockeying for positions of power and authority in the evolving and faction-ridden Bangladeshi set-up. The upshot was that he enjoyed the total trust, confidence and support of the entire Indian establishment. I had heard from various senior Indian officials including Lt Gen. B.N. Sarkar that Mrs Gandhi and her advisers thought Tajuddin had no alternative or an equal neither in his own party nor in the government nor outside. What had dismayed the Indian establishment the most was that the majority of Awami League leaders had started banking heavily more on Indian recognition and military intervention than waging a guerrilla war to achieve their Bangladesh goal. They wanted Bangladesh to be served to them on a platter. Most of those leaders failed to realize the international implications of India recognizing Bangladesh or going to war with Pakistan by marching its military into East Pakistan. That planning a war was no child's play and needed months of preparation never occurred to them. This was another sore point with Indian policy planners.

Mrs Gandhi's suggestion of forming a government in exile in the presence of international media suddenly provided a positive direction and the much-needed impetus to the liberation war effort. The first thing Tajuddin did after his meeting with Mrs Gandhi was to rush to Tura in Meghalaya in a Dakota aircraft provided by the BSF. There he met the Awami League stalwart Syed Nazrul Islam and proposed that he become the acting president of the government in exile. There was no provision for the post of acting president in the government that Mujib had formed. Tajuddin informed Nazrul Islam about his encouraging interactions with Mrs Gandhi, which enthused Nazrul Islam to join hands with Tajuddin as he grabbed the offer. Tajuddin went from one refugee camp to another to locate other senior Awami League leaders.

Since a government was already in place, Tajuddin did not face a serious problem in selecting ministers of the government in exile. It helped that most of them had crossed over to India and many had made Calcutta their temporary homes. The question was when and where the swearing-in ceremony would take place. This was of serious concern both for Tajuddin and the Indian government. The Pakistan military was desperately trying to regain control of territories where the Bangladesh flag was still flying and plug the gaps along India-East Pakistan border through which the *mukti*s were sneaking in and out at will to attack Pakistani positions. Initially, Chuadanga was selected as the venue for the swearing in but only a few days ago Pak Sabre jets had strafed the town. The jets had dropped Napalm bombs on the local EPR camp, wiping out the entire encampment. So Chuadanga was ruled out as a venue.

The Indian security establishment led by the BSF bosses, Rustamji and Golak, pored over the Bangladesh map to identify areas that were still under the control of the freedom fighters. Because of security and logistical reasons, the swearing-in venue had to be close to the Indian border and also connected by road to Calcutta so that the representatives of international media and the ministers to be sworn in could be easily, directly and quietly driven there by cars straight from Calcutta. After a painstaking review of the maps both by Rustamji and Golak and with Tajuddin's approval, they zeroed in on an area jutting into Indian territory, which was surrounded on three sides by the Nadia district of West Bengal. The area known as Baidyanathtala near Meherpur town had a sprawling and dense mango grove, which would not only provide an excellent natural cover for the swearing-in function but was also considered an auspicious venue for the occasion as the intoxicating aroma of mango buds, already in full bloom, heavily filled the air.

Tawfiq-e-Elahi Chowdhury, SDO of Meherpur, reported that the Pak Army's march towards Meherpur had been halted by the determined resistance from the EBR, EPR and the *mukti* volunteers. The Pakis were still at a 'safe distance' but chances of strafing by Pak fighters were high. Whatever was to be done had to be done in total secrecy, fast and, of course, with 'adequate safeguards'. Rustamji and Golak swung into action instantly. The anti-aircraft guns of the army's air defence units were brought in and deployed around the mango grove only a few hours before the actual ceremony started so as not to arouse suspicion.

The public relations wing of the BSF, headed by Samar Bose, and that of the military, helmed by Col. I. Rikhye, accomplished the herculean task of locating all the foreign correspondents camping in Calcutta by calling on them individually in their hotel rooms and inviting them to reach Calcutta Press Club at 4 am on 17 April. They were told that from there they would be driven to an 'undisclosed destination', a term that aroused considerable curiosity among the foreign press corps. The national press corps too had been invited for the trip to the mysterious destination as were the Delhi-based Indian stringers of foreign papers and TV channels.

The media world was kept in high suspense and not given any details about what the proposed mysterious trip was about. This led to wild speculation. The then American consul general in Calcutta, Mr Griffin, and his political officer Mr Neqib Ahmed, and the British deputy high commissioner, were desperately trying to figure out what the early morning meeting of 17 April was all about. The Indian defence establishment had never ever conducted such a massive PR exercise either for Indian or visiting foreign journalists at such an odd hour. Significantly, this would also be the biggest ever assemblage of foreign journalists on Indian soil. Herding the media from all over the world was a stupendous task but performed with such great ease and aplomb that it won accolades from foreign journalists themselves.

There was a serious logistical problem though. How would Bose and Rikhye take well over 200 journalists from Calcutta in moderate comfort to a remote destination? Calcutta did not have private taxis in those days. However, there were private cars available on rent and at least 60 of them had to be hired for the purpose. Rustamji and Golak did not want to use them nor did they want to requisition such a huge number of government cars for this purpose because that would entail a bureaucratic rigmarole and certainly invite a breach of the total veil of secrecy, under which the swearing-in ceremony was to be conducted.

Once again, Golak Majumdar turned to Nihar Chakravarty for help. He wanted Nihar babu to arrange a fleet of 60 cars in very good condition, to ferry the press corps from Calcutta to the desired destination. Nihar babu approached his friends and well-wishers in his business circle to lend their cars with their 'trusted' drivers for a day because he could not trust strangers driving those cars going on a sensitive mission. The drivers were not told which route they would be taking after departing from the Press Club. They were just told to follow the VVIP convoy. The Pakistani spy ring, then run from the Pakistan Deputy High Commission in Calcutta, had suddenly become very active, resulting in quite a few arrests.

Rustamji and Golak Majumdar led the motorcade of VVIP guests, including those who were to be sworn in, under a thick cover of heavily armed commandos. When the motorcade reached Kalyani, it had become clear to Indian correspondents, myself included, that it was heading for the Indo-Bangladesh border. Whenever the motorcade stopped on the way, Barrister Amirul Islam was seen deeply engrossed in reading a written text over and over again. It was the final draft of the Declaration of Independence that he had prepared on Tajuddin Ahmed's orders.

While both Rustamji and Golak were busy working out the nitty gritties of security details of the swearing-in ceremony, two junior Bengali diplomats of the Pakistan High Commission in Delhi, K.M. Shahbuddin, second secretary, and Amzadul Haq, assistant press attaché, defected and pledged their allegiance to the Bangladesh government in exile. They were in for great inhuman indignities at the hands of their non-Bengali colleagues of the Pakistani mission. They were literally stranded on the streets with nowhere to go. Their personal belongings were thrown out on the streets by the non-Bengali staff. Senior Indian Bengali journalists like Dilip Mukherjee and Nikhil Chakravarty went to their rescue and put them up and their families at their homes for quite some time.

A Diplomatic Coup

There was an ongoing drama on two fronts. Even as they were facilitating the declaration of a government in exile, Rustamji and Golak hit upon an idea of engineering a large-scale defection of the Bengali staff of Pakistan's Calcutta-based Deputy High Commission headed by a Bengali career diplomat, Hossain Ali. They established contact with him and other Bengali staff of the mission but they were too scared to defect because of their personal safety and security concerns and also for financial reasons. Golak wanted an en masse defection of the Bengali staff, both diplomatic and non-diplomatic. Thus, when they defected, by virtue of their strength, they could at once take charge of the entire mission compound and make it extremely difficult for the non-Bengali staff to function or put up any kind of resistance.

Hossain Ali, however, nursed a nagging fear of being physically attacked by his non-Bengali colleagues. He was also scared of the non-Bengali residents of Park Circus, many of whom he suspected to be on the payroll of the Pakistanis. They would not allow him and his Bengali staff to step out of the mission. Golak assured Hossain Ali that he would put the mission under a thick security cover of BSF commandos to instil a sense of security among the would-be defectors. Both Rustamji and he would be outside the mission with a large force, the day Hossain Ali and the Bengali members of the staff defected and hoisted the Bangladesh flag atop the mission building.

If the plan was executed successfully, it would have a ripple effect on Pakistan's Bengali diplomats stationed worldwide.

The bosses, especially the babus, of the External Affairs Ministry (MEA) in Delhi got wind of the Rustamji-Golak plan and told them to nix it. The MEA did not like the BSF big guns meddling in the defection game, because the BSF was encroaching on the MEA's turf and supposedly understood very little about the intricacies of international diplomacy. Any faux pas would land India in serious trouble. However the defection plan had gone so far ahead by now that it was not possible to roll it back without putting the lives of Hossain Ali and his Bengali staff and their careers in serious jeopardy. Hossain Ali was also concerned about paying the salaries of his defecting staff. Golak assured him that his concern would be addressed without any problem. He got in touch with his friend Mr Baxi, the secretary in charge of banking services, in Delhi's Finance Ministry for help. Help came instantly.

The friend informed Golak that his ministry had the powers to 'freeze and seize' the Pak mission's 'massive account' in India held with the American Express Bank in US dollars and other hard currencies. This would be done the day Hossain Ali and his Bengali staff defected. Both Rustamji and Golak suggested 18 April as the D-Day for defection, a day after the installation of the government in exile at Baidyanathtala. Hossain Ali immediately agreed to the date because he had heard rumours that he along with other Bengali staff would soon be transferred back to foreign office in Islamabad. The full-fledged support that Rustamji and Golak got from the PMO helped them to proceed with Hossain Ali's defection a day after the Baidyanathtala ceremony.

Meanwhile, the long VVIP motorcade reached Baidyanathtala at around 11 am on 17 April. It was evident that a momentous event was to be staged there. A massive security ring of heavily armed BSF commandos in civvies had been thrown around the entire mango grove. They had taken up positions behind the trunks of mango trees. Ack-Ack gun crews were manning their respective stations. The IAF jets were hovering over in nearby Bongaon and Kalyani skies in case Pak jets came to attack the venue, which was barely few hundred yards from the Indian border at Nadia. Some members of the foreign media alighted from their cars and started asking the Bangladeshi VVIPs why they had been brought to such a 'god-damned back of beyond place' after an arduous drive of seven hours. Some sarcastically asked: 'Have you brought us to see this mango grove and how mangoes are grown here?' I still remember Tawfiq telling one American correspondent to 'have patience and to wait for a dramatic announcement to be made soon'.

A small motlcy contingent of EPR, police and *ansars* in tattered khaki uniform with no berets on their head, was rehearsing the guard of honour drill in one corner of the mango grove. In another corner, a musical group, without any musical instrument, was practising Bangladesh's national anthem '*Aamaar Sonar Bangla*' in all earnestness. Golak was suddenly asked to procure a tabla and harmonium from the neighbouring Indian villages. Without musical accompaniment, the national anthem was not sounding vibrant or even sonorous enough. A battery-operated sound system was still being installed and tested. A makeshift platform made of wooden *takhtaposh* (low, wooden table-like platform) with seven or eight chairs on it stood out conspicuously alongside a flagpole made from a freshly cut bamboo, which had a wrapped Bangladesh flag tied to its mast. Tawfiq was busy adding last-minute finishing touches. Both Rustamji and Golak stayed on the Indian side of the border leaving it to the Bangladeshis to manage and call this historic show their very own. They were heard telling the Bangladeshi managers of the ceremony to 'hurry up' as they had to rush back to Calcutta where, 'very urgent pending matters awaited their attention'. Except Tajuddin no one knew what those 'urgent pending matters' were.

The mango grove was teeming with curious crowds from both sides of the border, waiting with bated breath for the ceremony to start. Onlookers had climbed giant banyan trees and precariously perched themselves on branches to get a better view of the event. It was only when the Awami League leadership led by Nazrul Islam and Tajuddin Ahmed got on to the stage one by one that it became clear that the Bangladesh government was being formally installed to cover which the international media had been invited. When the Awami League MNA from Dinajpur, Prof. Yusuf Ali, took the stage and started reading the Proclamation of Independence on the mike, it was the first formal and official announcement from the Bangladesh government in exile, declaring Bangladesh an independent sovereign people's republic.

While bestowing the independent status on Bangladesh, Sheikh Mujib had in his declaration of independence message delivered on the midnight of 25 March, just before his arrest, called upon the Bengalis to fight the Pakistanis until total victory had been achieved. His message was still echoing in the hearts and minds of many in the vast crowd, especially those who had heard his declaration message on the radio. Prof. Ali informed the gathering that Bangladesh's Independence had taken effect from 25 March itself. He further announced that the proclamation that he was reading provided the fundamental instrument of law as well as an interim Constitution of the government in exile, henceforth to be known as Mujib Nagar Government. Baidyanathtala had already been renamed as Mujib Nagar at the meeting of the MNAs soon after their arrival at the mango grove that morning. The interim Constitution would be in force during the entire period of liberation war and, of course, until such time that a full-fledged Constitution was adopted by a liberated Bangladesh.

The next announcement was that the duly elected MNAs and MPAs had met on 10 April in Calcutta and had formed themselves into a constituent assembly in exile for drafting the declaration of independence. A formal meeting of that assembly in exile had been held at Mujib Nagar that morning, where it was decided that the constituent assembly would be the supreme and sovereign authority of Bangladesh, under whose command and direction the liberation war would be fought. Then, as a duly-constituted potentiary, Prof. Ali administered the oath of office to Syed Nazrul Islam as Acting President of Bangladesh. To the singing of the national anthem the Bangladesh flag was unfurled.

These historic scenes electrified the vast gathering. They raised the '*Joy Bangla*' slogan with such gusto that it reverberated in the air of the entire Baidyanathtala. The acting president, Syed Nazrul Islam, was given a guard of honour by those who were seen rehearsing in the morning. As the guard presented arms, another round of resounding cries of '*Joy Bangla*' rented the air. Syed Nazrul along with his prime minister, Tajuddin Ahmed, and five other ministers, posed for photographs for the press. Flashbulbs popped ceaselessly and the whirring sound of dozens of rolling TV cameras of foreign electronic media brought a sense of fulfilment to the Bangladeshi leaders. Their event would get global news coverage next morning.

The next morning the whole world came to know the *raison d' être* of Bangladesh's freedom struggle along with the message that, unlike the Biafran episode, it would not be a flash in the pan, only to end up in a fiasco. Both Rustamji and Golak were elated that their closely coordinated exercise with the government in exile had paid off. The Bangladesh leadership had successfully passed a major milestone in their march towards liberating their country. It was the first major test that both sides could work together in perfect harmony. The Indian dailies, English or vernacular, gave a detailed coverage of the event with stories and pictures. It seemed as if it was more a national than an international event.

Undoubtedly, both Rustamji and Golak had been able to successfully project to the whole world, through the international media, the positive side of the Bangladesh struggle at the swearing-in ceremony. An elected, legitimate government in exile, unlike the Biafran revolt, having legal and wide popular support, was responsible for waging a just liberation war against the Pakistanis. On their return trip to Calcutta they had decided that they should jointly wage an offensive on the diplomatic front as well and spring another surprise on the Pakistanis. On their return to the city they got in touch with Hossain Ali late at night to reconfirm his defection plan.

Hossain Ali was too scared to take the big decisive leap. He was afraid of a reprisal including physical attacks on him, his wife and the Bengali staff. It took Golak several rounds of persuasion to convince him that a positive response from his side would be a giant leap forward, which would work as a catalyst in setting off large-scale defection amongst the Bengali diplomatic and non-diplomatic staff posted in Pakistani missions abroad. Golak pepped up Hossain Ali's morale by saying he wanted the Bengali staff of the Pakistani mission in Calcutta to become the role model for the other Bengali staff in Pak missions overseas and turn the Calcutta mission compound into a busy hub of all diplomatic activities of the government in exile, which had already camped itself in the city.

Throughout the night, Rustamji and Golak meticulously worked out their foolproof plan and made their presence felt outside the Pak Deputy High Commission from the dawn of 18 April. They needed to ensure that the defection and hoisting of the Bangladesh flag happened smoothly. Golak had stationed himself on the footpath, bang opposite the main gate of the Pakistani mission with a small wooden box stacked with shoe brushes, boot polish bottles and polish containers. He wore a soiled *kurta* (loose shirt) and a skullcap on his head and put on a typical Muslim whisker on his face. Occasionally, he would plead passers-by to get their shoes polished for Re 1 ('*Ek rupai may joota polish karwa lo*') in Hindi.

Golak Majumdar as the *bootpolishwala* (shoe-shiner) was so perfect that even Rustamji, who had disguised himself as a morning walker, failed to spot him. He had walked past him at least a dozen times that morning. In fact, unable to locate him Rustamji got anxious and asked about his whereabouts. He was told that Golak Sir was very much around and on duty but Rustamji still could not locate him. Both saw Hossain Ali along with his wife and a large number of Bengali staff (65 in all) of the mission, reaching the roof of the mission building and hoisting the Bangladesh flag amid cries of '*Joy Bangla*'. Soon a large crowd gathered outside the mission and they too ended up shouting the '*Joy Bangla*' war cry.

In a historic and momentous event, the Bangladesh flag was officially unfurled on foreign soil. The Calcutta station of All India Radio broadcast the news, which made Calcuttans, including numerous celebrities, especially singers, converge on the Bangladesh mission in thousands. A makeshift stage and *shamiana* (tent) were put up where patriotic Bengali songs were sung throughout the day in front of a vast gathering. The doors of the mission were thrown open and crowds got in to congratulate Hossain Ali and his Bengali staff for their courage and unwavering loyalty to the cause of Bangladesh. In no time, this first Bangladesh mission overseas turned into Tajuddin Ahmed's government in exile's first foreign office. As envisaged by Rustamji and Golak Majumdar, what happened in Calcutta on 18 April triggered a large-scale defection of the Bengali diplomats at the UN headquarters in New York and in major capitals of the world.

The PMO was happy that Rustamji and Golak had quietly pulled off a diplomatic coup, which had not only strengthened the hands and boosted the morale of the government in exile and that of the freedom fighters but also contributed handsomely to Pakistan's diplomatic discomfiture globally.

Slaughtering Secularism

General Yahya was stung. The formation of a government in exile under the full glare of global media and the large-scale defection of Pakistan's Bengali diplomats, shifting their allegiance to the Mujib Nagar government overnight was beyond his wildest nightmares. The immediate response was to send massive reinforcements by air and sea to East Pakistan to beef up its garrisons there for launching an all-out military offensive against the Mukti Bahini. The worsening situation in the eastern wing made him send personal emissaries to address the mess at a diplomatic level on the one hand. They went to major capitals of the world to explain the initiatives that he was taking to restore normalcy. On the other, he went on an all-out military offensive to steamroll the Mukti Bahini's citadels of resistance in the outlying districts like Kushtia, Rajshahi and pockets in Sylhet, Mymensingh, Comilla and Chittagong, which the *mukti*s were still holding on to.

Chittagong, Chuadanga and Rajshahi, centres offering dour resistance, were strafed by his Sabre jets. To enforce his gruesome plan, he sent Lt Gen. A.A.K. Niazi, one of his most decorated officers, to Dacca as the commander of East Pakistan's Eastern Command, to take over from Lt Gen. Tikka Khan. Tikka Khan had earned much international notoriety for the ruthless Operation Searchlight offensive of 25 March. His new nickname was the 'Butcher of Bengal'. General Niazi, who took charge from him on 4 April, considered

Bengalis of all religions to be 'low-lying people of low-lying land, who were worse than vermin and deserved total extermination'. His blinding hatred for Bengalis made him justify their massacre as he openly ventilated his feelings at staff meetings and when addressing his troops. The only effective way to save East Pakistan from the 'evil Indian influence was by mercilessly killing all the Hindus and their secular Muslim brothers, as they were their agents'.

Such pronouncements found their way to us across the border through the various sector commanders, who had their close Bengali buddies still serving in the Pak military establishment. 'Operation Searchlight' had sharply polarized the Bengali and non-Bengali officers and men, both in the military and civil services on linguistic and racial lines. Everything the Punjabi officers said and did got relayed to us in no time. Presiding over a meeting of his commanders, Niazi told his shell-shocked audience that he had 'issued written orders giving full freedom to his officers and men to kill as many Hindus as possible [exact words used were "*Kafir* extermination"] for which they would not be held accountable'. Like the brown shirts of the Nazis, who identified Jewish houses with crosses marked on their doors, Niazi ordered the *razakar*s (militia composed mostly of Biharis) and members of military-backed 'peace committees' to mark Hindu homes and shops with yellow paint so that they could be identified easily and their owners killed.

What the Jews were to Hitler, the Hindus were to Niazi. He would ask his troops to keep a count of how many Hindus they had killed every day, so that a grand official tally could be worked out at month's end. That would give a clear idea of how many Hindus they had been able to wipe out from the face of East Pakistan. Thus were his troops exhorted to '... kill whosoever Hindu comes your way. The problem of the Bengali Muslims is that they are Hindu at heart so they are a treacherous lot. Our war is between us (pure) and them (impure Muslims). The Bengali problem requires a military and not a political solution.' The Pakistan army chief, General Hamid Khan, while inspecting his troops in East Pakistan in 1971, would ask his soldiers: '*Jawan, tumne aajtak kitne Hindu maare*?' (Soldier, how many Hindus have you killed till date?) The Bengali women, irrespective of religion and age, were considered by him to be '*gonimat ka maal*' (public property), which should first be enjoyed and then killed without fail and at will with no questions asked. At one meeting of commanders, Niazi had even openly vowed to change the Bengali *nasal* (race) altogether. This upset one Bengali Major Mushtaq present at the meeting so much that he went to the toilet and shot himself to death with his service revolver. This incident finds mention in Lt Gen. Khadim Hussain Raja's book *A Stranger in My Own Country* (2012).

Hindus, thus, accounted for about 75 per cent of the refugees entering India in ever growing numbers; between 55,000 and 60,000 coming in every day at the tail end of April, with women in the majority. There was another category of Bengalis, mostly Muslim youths and peasants, who mingled with the refugees and entered India in large numbers. During my almost daily visits to Boyra, Tehatta and Gede borders to cover the refugee influx, I could see their steadily growing numbers, which convinced me about the positive outcome of the liberation war. Many, whom I met at the border, were college students from faraway places, including Dacca and other towns. On crossing over, they would urgently ask for the location of the nearest Mukti Bahini camp or the BSF outpost. If I asked them why, their reply was that they were here for training in arms to join the Mukti Bahini and rid the country of the *Khan Sena* (Pak military). Except for the ragged bags hanging from their shoulders, containing a set of clothes and red *gamchcha*s (towels) strung around their neck or head, they carried nothing else. They were usually barefooted and wore a sleeveless *banyan* (vest) or a shirt and a *lungi*. They looked and sounded committed to the cause that had driven them to crossing the border to India.

A vast majority was from the peasant stock, mostly unlettered. I was in awe of their conviction in the cause of liberation of their land from the Pakistani yoke. They said that youths from their neighbouring villages had already crossed over to India in hundreds to take arms training and participate in the liberation war. More were waiting in the wings. Broadcasts from the Swadhin Bangla Betar Kendro and All India Radio had spurred them on to join the freedom struggle voluntarily. Their parents were equally committed to the cause and did not stop their sons from coming to India. They actually egged them on to join the Mukti Bahini. Significantly, every volunteer swore by Sheikh Mujib and his call for independence. On several occasions, I had taken them in my office car and dropped them off at youth camps. There were 25 of them functioning along the border, enlisting youths as recruits for the Mukti Bahini.

Late April was also when the Opposition leaders in the Indian Parliament demanded the recognition of the government in exile and an Indian military intervention in Bangladesh. Indira Gandhi and her advisers rejected them saying that the time was far from ripe for taking those crucial decisions. She argued that a military intervention would boomerang on India and subvert the process of the liberation war, which had attracted international attention, especially after the swearing in of the provisional government. According to her, any Indian intervention would be construed as part of Indian conspiracy to dismember Pakistan, a point which Pakistan was trying to sell to the outside world without much success. Any such action would only justify the Pakistani stand. India had to tread cautiously because Bangladesh had suddenly become the focus of international diplomacy and attention because of the on-going popular pro-democracy movement there.

General Yahya's counter and false narrative, propagated by his personal emissaries in various global capitals, was that the civil-war-like situation, created by the secessionists in East Pakistan, had been 'controlled' with the arrest of its 'ring leader' and the 'real villain of the piece' – Sheikh Mujib. His story was that 'normalcy was fast returning to the disturbed province because of the positive initiatives taken by him'. He assured world leaders that, once normalcy was restored, he would begin negotiations with the elected members of the National Assembly for an amicable solution. He claimed significant progress with establishing contact with many MNAs, who were part of the 'so-called provisional government'. He found it encouraging that they had 'positively responded to his peace and normalcy initiatives' and even expressed explicit willingness to return to Dacca for talks whenever asked to.

An immediate offshoot of the government in exile, working out of Calcutta, and the massive refugee influx was that the city became the hub of international news and diplomacy overnight. Visitors included world VVIPS such as UN Secretary General Kurt Waldheim, the head of the United Nations High Commissioner of Refugees, Prince Sadruddin Aga Khan, American senators, including Ted Kennedy, French Culture Minister Andre Malraux, Soviet Deputy Foreign Minister V.V. Kuznetsov, and high-profile British MPs like John Stonehouse, apart from many Nobel laureates. They were flying in and out of the city almost daily to see first-hand and gauge the enormity of the refugee crisis that was swamping India.

The Indian external affairs ministry had opened its branch secretariat in the city headed by a seasoned Bengali diplomat, Ashoke Roy, a senior joint secretary in the MEA. It took me some time to cultivate him and win his confidence. I went to him regularly for informal briefings at his sprawling Ballygunje Park Road office. He became one of my news sources, especially with regard to behind-the-scene diplomacy pertaining to Bangladesh.

The foreign missions in the city, especially the American, Soviet and the British, had also beefed up the political and intelligence wings of their missions significantly. The most eye-catching and active diplomats were those from the American and Soviet consulates but Gurginov and the KGB head of the Soviet Consulate were the most-high profile of them all. They kept close tabs on Bangladesh-oriented developments in the city. Gurginov was a frequent visitor to the Calcutta Press Club and was on first name terms with many senior Calcutta-based correspondents largely because he could converse with them in fluent and chaste Bengali, usually spoken by Calcutta Bengalis. This endeared him to them the most. He was also one of my sources.

It was he who first tipped me off that diplomats of the American consulate, including the consul general himself, a certain Mr Griffin, were in touch with some Awami League MNAs and were wooing them to go back to Dacca to work out a settlement with Yahya without Mujib at the negotiating table. Moscow took little notice of Yahya, whose emissary to Moscow apprised the Kremlin leaders that the Pak president was trying his best to restore normalcy in East Pakistan and that the Soviets should desist from extending any kind of moral or material support to the provisional government under pressure from India. The Soviet leadership gave the emissary a patient hearing and was extremely cautious in its interaction with him. The emissary went back empty handed with no pledge of support from the Soviet leaders for the Pakistani stand.

Yahya had, of course, scored with the Americans. The MNAs, who had been wooed over with help from the American consulate, belonged to the Khondokar Mushtaq Ahmed camp. Khondokar was the foreign minister of the provisional government and had committed followers in the bureaucracy of the Mujib Nagar government. For the time being, a close watch on them by the sleuths of the Research and Analysis Wing (RAW) frustrated their efforts to respond positively to Yahya's game plan. Yahya had, however, been able to identify those in the Awami League-led provisional government who could play the role of a Trojan horse in future and help him derail the 'so-called liberation war' with the help of the American consulate in Calcutta. Although Yahya's move did not succeed then, it marked the beginning of the process to take Bangladesh in the reverse direction. Four years later, it culminated in the dastardly killing of Sheikh Mujib and almost his entire family along with four senior leaders of the Awami League.

Chinese Frowns and Soviet Nods

Yahya's Kremlin setback was on account of his narrative being diametrically opposite to the reports that the Kremlin was receiving from its diplomats in Dacca and Islamabad. There was no sign of normalcy returning to Dacca and the rest of the country as large-scale killing by the military was continuing to obliterate the last vestiges of resistance. Significantly, after the emissary's departure, the Kremlin responded positively to Indira Gandhi's appeal for help for logistical support to deal with the worsening refugee crisis. It announced the dispatch of a fleet of transport aircraft with its crew and ground support staff and equipment to Calcutta to ferry the excess refugees, who were overflowing their camps in and around Calcutta, to the new ones set up in Madhya Pradesh.

The end of April and early May was also when the Bangladesh issue had become a major pawn in the chessboard of international diplomacy and polemical battles. China was the first major power to make a move by openly warning India 'not to meddle in Pakistan's domestic affairs'. If it did so, it would 'burn its fingers' and have to 'rue and pay a heavy price'. China's open threat to India caught the attention of all Indians, especially the Leftists of West Bengal. What sounded very odd to us was that the Chinese made no mention of the mass killings that Pakistan had resorted to, setting off history's biggest ever exodus of refugees into India, thereby besetting it with gargantuan problems that were divisive in nature and threatening its progress and national security. Instead of empathizing with India, Peking stepped up its arms supply to Pakistan and informed Pakistan's Bengali envoy, Khwaja Mohammed Kaiser, that it had already issued a veiled threat to India that it would intervene if the situation warranted it.

Not to be outdone, on 3 April, Soviet President Nikolai Podgorny delivered an ultimatum to Yahya to 'immediately stop the genocide', making headlines in all Calcutta dailies. On 17 April, Soviet Premier Alexei Kosygin followed this up with a message to Yahya urging him to peacefully negotiate a political settlement with the stakeholders. He had stressed that any settlement must take into account the 'lawful wishes of the parties involved in the crisis. Also, the interests of populations of both East and West Pakistan should be factored into consideration for finding a solution' (as reported by Russian News Agency TASS). Gurginov informed us that Kremlin, of course, had serious doubts about Yahya's ability to work out such a solution and restore peace and normalcy in East Pakistan because it was aware of the mindset of the regime that Yahya represented and also of the on-going genocide in East Pakistan.

Kremlin's apprehension had been conveyed to Mrs Gandhi's advisers by the then Soviet envoy in Delhi, Nikolay Pegov. The Soviet leadership suspected that the Chinese were in favour of prolonging instability in East Pakistan as that would help them to make significant political inroads into the region in their bid to spread their influence in East Pakistan's troubled situation. The Chinese, who were hell-bent on subverting the liberation war and spreading chaos and confusion in the region, were supporting their stooges in East Pakistan. The Soviet leadership concurred with the Indian assessment that prolonging the liberation war might help the armed Naxalite radicals to infiltrate and take control of the liberation war by resorting to political subterfuge.

Declassified Indian archival records reveal that even the Soviet defence minister, Marshal Grechko, had told the then Indian envoy in Moscow, D.P. Dhar, many times that the threat to India's security was not so much from Pakistan, which Delhi could handle on its own. It was graver from its 'unpredictable and dubious northern' neighbour, China. Grechko had suggested to Dhar that 'some kind of treaty of friendship and co-operation' between India and the Soviet Union, would be a 'good preventive measure against Chinese and Pakistani aggression against India'. In Marshal Grechko's assessment, India being militarily weak would not be able to cope if both West Pakistan and China launched simultaneous attacks against it. The same treaty proposal had been conveyed to Mrs Gandhi's advisers by the Soviet envoy in Delhi, Nikolay Pegov. The then Indian foreign minister, Sardar Swaran Singh, was lukewarm to the idea, leading to a stalemate for the time being.

Gurginov had said Peking's desperation to forcibly grab the Ussuri river islands in Siberia had opened Moscow's eyes to China's expansionist design and game. This Soviet assessment coincided with that of the Indian security establishment, which considered the manifestations of the violent Naxalite movement in parts of eastern India and its efforts to tie up with the Marxist-Leninist groups of East Pakistan as a precursor to Chinese intervention in the region. A group of top Naxalite leaders had already visited Peking secretly and met the senior leaders of the Chinese Communist Party for help and support. The Naga and Mizo insurgents, operating in India's north-east from their staging posts in East Pakistan, were also in touch with Peking and were being funded and armed by the Chinese to foment an armed insurrection in India's north-east. This posed an equally serious threat to India's security.

This assessment of China's possible involvement in the East Pakistan imbroglio impelled Mrs Gandhi's policy planners to provide an all-out support to the Bangladesh liberation war effort. India's total support to the liberation war was guided by its national security interests, which meant it had to give shape and substance to the Bengali nationhood in the shortest possible time. It pursued this objective with single-minded devotion though China was firing salvo after salvo in its polemical battle against the Soviets. Peking's position was that 'Soviet revisionist and social imperialist' forces were in cahoots with 'arch Indian reactionaries, running dogs of the Kremlin' trying to invade and annex East Pakistan in their bid to set up a 'puppet regime there, in so-called' Bangladesh. Peking's salvo was in response to Soviet President Nikolai Podgorny's statement of 3 April, calling upon Yahya to 'immediately stop committing genocide in Bangladesh'.

Almost at the same time, Indira Gandhi demanded an end to Pakistan's mass killings in Bangladesh in a shriller tone both inside and outside Indian Parliament. Peking's provocative reaction to Podgorny's appeal and Indira Gandhi's speech were not unexpected. It was still smarting under the humiliation of its PLA units getting a bloody nose from the Red Army for trying to take control of disputed islands on the Ussuri river in 1969. What further motivated the Chinese to make such a patently combative anti-Soviet and anti-India pronouncement was that they were desperately trying to improve their relations with the US.

The Chinese Communist Party leaders hoped that their anti-Soviet and anti-India blast would please President Nixon. The American president was at that time trying to build bridges of understanding with them and, according to declassified White House papers, had a 'total dislike' for Indira Gandhi, whom he considered to be a 'Soviet stooge'. For her father, he had 'nothing but scorn and an intense personal aversion'. Besides, as those documents reveal, he harboured racial prejudice against Indian women. The Chinese leaders had also noticed that President Nixon and his National Security Adviser Henry Kissinger had refrained from joining the international condemnation of the gross excesses committed by the Pak military in East Pakistan. The Chinese leadership felt that the best way to tune in to the American line and cozy up to White House was by launching a virulent anti-Soviet and anti-India tirade. Given China's national interest, this was very much in order, even if it compromised its ideological moorings.

It is very pertinent to mention here that at a time when no Bangladeshi leader was daring to take on the Chinese leadership for their nefarious anti-Bangladesh role, it was Maulana Bhasani, leader of a pro-China faction of NAP, who had the temerity to dispatch scathing telegrams to Mao and Zhou Enlai, openly questioning them about their socialist and communist credentials for not standing by the oppressed people of Bangladesh. In his telegram, the contents of which he shared with some Calcutta journalists including myself, sent in the third week of April he wrote, 'If your government does not condemn the brutal atrocities committed by the Pakistani military junta with the support of vested interests of West Pakistan, the world may think you are no longer the friend of oppressed people of the world.' About the same time, a much-respected and noted literary icon of Dacca, Shaukat Osman, who had sought shelter in Calcutta, in an open letter addressed to the Chinese Communist Party leaders posed almost identical questions that Bhasani had asked but with such great literary panache and finesse that local Calcutta dailies could not but help publish it. Bhasani had sent the telegram after he came to Calcutta in mid-April and had held discussions with Tajuddin in this regard. But it evoked no reaction, not even an acknowledgement from the Chinese Communist Party.

A World Antagonized

Although the barbarities committed by the Pak military against the unarmed Bengalis had evoked international condemnation and sympathy and support for the Bangladesh cause, most countries, including non-Islamic ones, were opposing the liberation war, as they firmly upheld the principles of national sovereignty and territorial integrity which, according to them, were sacrosanct and inviolate. Those principles also formed an inseparable part of international law, justice and practice. Many world leaders had privately conveyed their concern to Indira Gandhi and other Indian leaders that lending support to the Bangladesh Liberation War would 'most certainly encourage' separatists waging secessionist movements in their own countries and eventually lead to their dismemberment.

Leaders of countries like Yugoslavia, United Arab Republic and Indonesia (Marshall Tito, Gamal Abdel Nasser and Suharto), who were the main pillars of the non-aligned bloc, had made known their strong reservations against the Bangladesh movement to India. Ashoke Roy, head of MEA's branch secretariat in Calcutta, amongst the many distinguished Indian diplomats sent overseas to garner diplomatic support and mobilize international public opinion in favour of the provisional government, explained to me the mindset of global leaders. India hit a wall, when it took upon itself the diplomatic role of explaining to the world the righteous cause of the Bangladesh struggle. Many world leaders were not willing to hear about the 'bloody subversion of democracy' by the Pakistani rulers as they themselves did not believe in democratic norms. Most foreign ministers of countries that he had visited initially had refused to hear the Bangladesh side of the story. Fed on Pak propaganda, they were not convinced that the Pak military had unleashed genocide in East Pakistan.

They had to be shown pictures of mass killings by the Pak military and the hellish living condition of Indian camps overflowing with refugees to convince them that terror-struck Bengalis of East Pakistan were voluntarily fleeing their home and hearth to escape genocide and rape and seek shelter in Indian refugee camps in hundreds of thousands. 'Why would they come to India to live in such pitiable conditions?' Roy had argued with them. Even at the risk of incurring the displeasure of the foreign minister of an Islamic country, Roy politely reminded him that there was so much diplomatic hullabaloo by the leaders of the Islamic bloc over the plight of 1.5 million Palestinian refugees, living in camps spread in five countries of West Asia, whereas India alone had to bear the brunt of almost 7 million refugees; their numbers rapidly growing every day, with no prospect of their returning home in the near future. He was shocked by the blunt comment of that west Asian foreign minister: 'According to my information most of the refugees are non-Muslims. You are a Hindu-majority country. So they have come to India. Why should you be bothered? We are not bothered about their and your plight.'

Another seasoned diplomat drafted for this purpose was Syed Shahbuddin, who had told me that presidents and prime ministers of even far-off Latin American countries had expressed their misgivings about the Bangladesh struggle, as their own countries were already beset with secessionist movements. If the Bangladesh struggle succeeded, it would provide stimulus to them. They had no answer when Shahbuddin had countered, the Mexican president, for instance, by asking if suppressing a popular mandate with ruthless military action, causing death to hundreds of thousands of unarmed civilians, was the right answer to stonewall the popular will of the people? Such a step would not only give a shot-in-the-arm to secessionist forces but also provide *raison d'être* to their secessionist strategy and set in motion the irreversible processes of armed struggle.

Shahbuddin had cited various social and armed political movements in Mexico and pointed out that the Mexican government's response to them was not genocidal. On the contrary, the response was neo-liberal in character, which was helping to defuse the situation. Like Syed Shahbuddin, Indian diplomats stationed in numerous missions the world over, had persistently allayed apprehensions of various government leaders with persuasive arguments to set at rest their fears of political and social consequences for supporting Bangladesh's struggle for independence.

The silent, behind-the-scenes and relentless diplomatic moves by the Indian envoys to secure support for Bangladesh's cause is little known. Unfortunately, they do not even figure anywhere in Bangladesh's history books. At a time when the world's two biggest democracies, the US and the UK, were openly discounting the Pak Army's atrocities and not condemning General Yahya for refusing to keep his commitment to lift martial law and restore democracy by handing over power to a party which had secured an overwhelming popular mandate, the Indian envoys were single-handedly projecting and promoting the Bangladesh case. No one else was willing to plead forcefully on Bangladesh's behalf on the world stage. It was this monumental spadework that gradually helped change the perception of the non-Islamic, anti-Bangladesh lobby, vociferously opposing the liberation war of the Bengalis because of their own domestic compulsions. Both Roy and Shahbuddin said that almost 70 per cent of UN members opposed an independent Bangladesh around

March 1971. They included Ceylon, Burma, Indonesia and Malaysia among others. It was the phenomenal effort by those Indian envoys that made the uphill job of Justice Abu Sayeed Chowdhury, special envoy of the provisional Mujib Nagar government, to mobilize world opinion in Bangladesh's favour so much easier.

What had also greatly helped the Indian envoys and subsequently Justice Abu Sayeed Chowdhury in launching their diplomatic offensive was the feedback that the major world capitals were getting from their diplomatic missions in Dacca, Delhi and Calcutta. The French cultural minister, Andre Malraux, visiting Calcutta to see the enormity of the refugee crisis that India was facing, admitted that he had taken the first flight to Calcutta after reading a series of distressing diplomatic dispatches from the then consul general in Calcutta. He was recounting horrendous experiences of the refugees being forced to flee East Pakistan from Pakistan Army's planned policy of committing 'selective genocide' and rape. So incensed was Malraux that he decided to hold an impromptu press conference at the Salt Lake refugee camp itself, where he announced that, after hearing the shocking stories of Pak atrocities, he wanted to take up arms again and do what he did during the Spanish civil war by leading an international brigade to fight General Franco, whose footsteps General Yahya Khan was following. General Yahya was the modern version of General Franco of the 1930s, said Malraux; his comment making headlines in the international media the next day.

The monsoons set in early in 1971 aggravating problems on the refugee front. The rain waters had made conditions in the refugee camps hellish as camp after camp became veritable cesspools. The large-scale outbreak of cholera and a new strain of viral fever was the least of the problems. A highly contagious eye disease, conjunctivitis (nicknamed 'Joy Bangla'), hit the refugees and, in fact, spread to Calcutta. Every other Bengali had 'Joy Bangla'.

In essence, a humanitarian disaster of gigantic proportions had struck India's eastern and north-eastern states, which hosted the bulk of the 900 refugee camps. The size of the crisis that these states were facing could be gauged from the fact that in a small state like Tripura, the number of refugees was more than double its population. West Bengal's Nadia district, bordering Bangladesh, alone had 2.2 million refugees, though its own population was less than 2 million. The refugees poured into Tripura and Nadia day and night in ceaseless torrents.

Swamped by Refugees

The Indian officials entrusted with relief work felt utterly helpless. Their plight was best expressed by Col. P.N. Luthra (Retd), in overall charge of refugee relief operations: 'Such was the huge flow that almost every day we kept revising our arrangement for relief operations. If we were making fresh arrangements for 45,000 to 50,000 new arrivals by opening new camps, we found that at the end of the day almost 100,000 had actually arrived.' His arrangements went haywire, landing the officials in serious trouble. 'Frankly, we did not know how to address the problem. It was humanly impossible to cope with an ever-rising number. They could not be quantified in advance.'

Wherever the Pak Army moved in the Hindu-dominated countryside, 'they killed, raped, burnt and looted the villages flanking the roads, leaving a diabolic trail of death and destruction'. The result was that terrorized residents of neighbouring villages 'started heading for the nearest Indian border' in thousands, the exodus overwhelming India from end April until early June when the flow peaked before starting to ebb. The terror-struck, starving, hapless refugees, walking for days through slush and mud, 'had no energy left in them and just came to our camps and collapsed', Luthra explained. I still can distinctly recall him seeing off the last trainload of refugees to Faridpur from Petrapole border station in March 1972, speaking to me with such a deep sense of anguish about the plight of the refugees. Even after an interlude of almost half a century, his words keep ringing in my ears.

I visited many of the camps to understand the enormity of the problem and was awestruck to see the NGOs, Indian and foreign, going about their assigned relief work with zeal, equanimity and dexterity. The hopelessness of the situation seemed to catalyze them to raise the bar. It was their dedication for a suffering humanity that prevented those camps from turning into mass graveyards of almost 10 million ill-fated refugees. Most were from Hindu-concentrated districts of Faridpur, Khulna, Patuakhali and Barisal. Even in June, large-scale killings were continuing in the countryside and India was at its wits' end, dealing with the aftermath without the wherewithal to address a crisis of this magnitude, not even with the massive international help that was pouring in.

The relief provided by the United Nations High Commissioner for Refugees (UNHCR) was quite inadequate, and much talked about in diplomatic circles both in Delhi and Calcutta. There were open suggestions that this was deliberate because the then chairman of UNHCR, Prince Sadruddin Aga Khan, was 'very close' to the Pakistani establishment. The refugee camp at Salt Lake, East Calcutta, for instance, had over 500,000 refugees. Half of them were stricken with cholera and viral fever. This pestilence-stricken camp had earned global infamy because of large-scale deaths. Ted Kennedy was so anguished to see their plight that he took off his shoes and walked barefoot through ankle-deep slush and mud to see the inside of refugee shelters. He talked to the refugees through an interpreter and saw for himself how they were being given green coconut water as a substitute IV fluid for saline in a makeshift medical centre run by the renowned French NGO, Médecins Sans Frontières.

The French doctors at the centre told him that huge supplies of saline were coming almost daily from overseas supplemented by purchases from the Indian market, but they got over in no time because of the virulent outbreak of cholera and a viral fever. They were often forced to use the green coconut water as a substitute. The Indian government encouraged the foreign dignitaries not only to visit the Salt Lake camp but also those at neighbouring Kalyani, Haringhata in Nadia district, which billeted over 800,000 refugees. More than 10,000 refugees had died of cholera in those two camps, according to Dipak Ghosh, the then district magistrate of Nadia. He had narrated to me his harrowing experiences with the plight of refugees for whose survival he and his support staff battled day and night against insurmountable odds. While visiting the camps under his charge I was convinced about the ground reality of the deteriorating refugee scene.

In desperation, Mrs Gandhi shot off a personal letter to 40 heads of government about the distressing refugee scene explaining that India was saddled with an unprecedented humanitarian and economic crisis, which no other country of the world had ever experienced. Worse, the crisis was not of its making. Unless their return to their homes was assured, with safety, honour and security, India's own security would be in jeopardy. Instead of honouring his pledge to hand over power to those who had secured the popular mandate, a ruthless military dictator was unleashing blood-curdling atrocities on his people, forcing them to seek refuge in neighbouring India in numbers never seen before in human history. India did not have the resources to shelter, feed, clothe and deal with a humanitarian problem of unprecedented dimensions.

Yahya's Provocations

Her letter evoked a bleak response from the world community, particularly from the West and Pakistan. Instead, General Yahya made a provocative statement saying all those who had taken shelter in India were Indians and not refugees from East Pakistan. He alleged that it was a 'cleverly contrived stage-managed show to defame' him and his great Islamic country with rich history and traditions. He also made the snide remark: 'Like Indians, I can also engineer such an influx to hoodwink the world community into believing that Pakistan is faced with a serious refugee crisis.' All these comments were getting published in Indian dailies and the Indian public was fuming.

When Ted Kennedy returned home and was asked by American journalists about Yahya's comment, he remarked that he was not buying that line. The whole world knew who those refugees were. He was not sure whether Yahya was joking and that the world community, including the American people, would have to help India in its most trying time. Ted Kennedy also said that he would raise his voice in the Senate to highlight the crisis and help India out and demand cutting off all kinds of US aid to Pakistan, which was committing selective genocide in East Pakistan. Meanwhile, pressure was being mounted on Yahya internationally to take back the refugees. He opened a few transit camps near the border to receive the refugees but no one returned. An Oxfam observer stationed in Jessore told an American news agency that on a visit to those camps he had found them totally deserted except for the officials manning them and some stray dogs loitering inside. There were no returnees from India there.

By mid-May, all the citadels of resistance had crumbled before the juggernaut of the Pak military machine. The stage was set for the second phase of the liberation struggle. It was known that the resistance of the freedom fighters would not be able to withstand the Pak military's onslaught because of much superior firepower. That the freedom fighters could hold on to their citadels for so long was in itself a big surprise to all, including the Indian policy planners. Mrs Gandhi had wisely utilized this time to make key appointments, which would help her navigate her government's Bangladesh policy safely through tortuous times to the expected goal, both at the national and international levels. The most significant appointment she made was of Durga Prasad Dhar, popularly known as DP, who had just relinquished his charge as India's envoy to Moscow.

D.P. Dhar's easy and unrestricted access to the top Soviet leaders and his excellent equations with them had secured him a berth as the chairman of the Policy Planning Committee of the Ministry of External Affairs. This was a special body created exclusively to meet the diplomatic exigencies arising from the fluid and difficult Bangladesh situation. He was also made India's chief interlocutor to liaise with the leaders of the provisional government. DP's appointment signified that Indira Gandhi would be relying heavily on Kremlin leaders for support in dealing with the Bangladesh crisis. The other consideration for his appointment was that he, a Kashmiri Pandit, teamed up excellently with another Kashmiri Pandit, Indira Gandhi's principal private secretary, Parameshwar Narayan Haksar. Haksar was the main political strategist and chief architect of most of her path-breaking national and international policies, initiatives and programmes. With his staunchly Fabian outlook, he had an excellent rapport with DP and kept him fully apprised in Moscow, when he was the Indian envoy talking about the Bangladesh situation from the Indian perspective. So when DP assumed his new role, he was well versed with the issues that he would have to handle and felt comfortable in dealing with them.

Indira Gandhi and her advisers were otherwise active as well, especially Mr Haksar. They had held interminable rounds of discussions with Indian military strategists and also those from Bangladesh just to take measure of the Pak Army's Eastern Command's operational capabilities in the countryside. Fully aware of the severe operational limitations in the rural deltaic region of the country, criss-crossed by rivers, rivulets, canals and massive water bodies, they opted for raising a Bengali guerilla force, which would be trained by the Indian military's guerilla commanders at special camps to be set up for the purpose. They would be trained to wage a war against the Pak military to wear them down psychologically and militarily by resorting to guerilla tactics. Such a war, waged effectively and in a sustained manner for seven to eight months, would wreak havoc on the Pak military's morale and psyche as they would lose their will and heart to prolong their fight in defending East Pakistan. The guerilla attacks would also take a heavy toll on East Pakistan's vital installations and its lifeline.

Raising a *Bahini*

During his second meeting with Indira Gandhi in Delhi on 6 May, Tajuddin Ahmed had been clearly told that military intervention by India and recognition of his provisional government, were being parked for the present because they would be counter-productive for the liberation war itself. Instead, India had drawn up a strategy of raising a force composed wholly of Bengali youths, who had sought shelter in India, who would be trained in techniques for waging guerilla warfare inside Bangladesh. This was in consonance with Sheikh Mujib's expressed wish, conveyed to Mrs Gandhi's emissary in London in 1969, where he had gone for an appendicitis operation. Mujib had for long been preparing for such an eventuality.

Mr Ahmed was also advised to 'consolidate' the Bangladesh political leadership under one umbrella as they lacked political cohesion which was badly needed to navigate the tortuous course of the liberation war. All the senior leaders of the pro-Moscow oriented Communist Party of Bangladesh (CPB) and those of the National Awami Party (Muzaffar) – NAP(M) – who were already in India, had expressed their wish to be a part of a broad-based 'national' government, as opposed to an exclusive Awami League government, which would make its functioning more cohesive and widely acceptable to the Bengali masses. The suggestion found no favour with Mr Ahmed, who countered the Indian advice by saying that such a move would rob the provisional government of its legitimacy because the Mujib Nagar government comprised only the elected MNAs of the Awami League. They were elected for the specific purpose of framing the new Constitution and, therefore, their induction into the provisional government imparted the stamp of legality. Tajuddin's opposition also stemmed from the fact that agreeing to such a proposal might give rise to a revolt-like situation in the party which would be too difficult to handle.

The provisional government was an electorally backed entity, which could not be written off as an illegitimate government, like the one headed by Col. Ojukwu in the breakaway Nigerian province of Biafra. Tajuddin Ahmed was clear. No CPB and NAP(M) members could be inducted into the government because most of their candidates, who had contested the 7 December election in East Pakistan, had lost even their security deposits. Even the supreme leader of the pro-China faction of NAP, Maulana Bhasani himself, supported Tajuddin's stand saying that formation of a national government comprising leaders of political parties who had lost in the 1970 election, would give rise to problems akin to opening of a Pandora's box. Moreover Bhasani was aware that there were moves by his party leaders in Dacca to bring him home, from where he would be flown to London to be installed as the head of a counter government in exile. To the Maulana's credit, he scrapped the move, which would have subverted the legally formed Mujib Nagar government and created disunity in the rank and file of freedom fighters. It would amount to betraying the cause of the liberation war. What Tajuddin Ahmed did agree to was forming an all-party consultative committee, in which both the CPB and NAP(M) leaders like Moni Singh and Prof. Muzaffar Ahmed would play a leading role. Even the formation of the all-party consultative committee had generated tremendous heat among a large section of Awami League leaders and workers led by Mujib's nephew Sheikh Fazlul Haq Moni, who firmly believed that it was formed under intense pressure of the Indian and Soviet leadership without holding any discussion with the rank and file of the Awami League which provided the backbone to the freedom struggle. He even accused India of treating the two inconsequential pro-Soviet parties at par with the Awami League which was the mainstay of the Bangladesh movement.

At the 6 May meeting Mrs Gandhi, as told to me by Mr Haksar much later, made four strategic suggestions. 'Consolidation' of all resources, human, material and financial, brought over from across the border and their judicious use for enhancing the liberation war effort. Given pressures from Moscow, Haksar and Dhar had suggested a meaningful role for other pro-liberation forces like the CPB and NAP(M) in the Mujib Nagar government so that their positive energies could be fully utilized and channelized towards the 'total struggle' for liberation. She inquired from Tajuddin and her own officials whether her order for opening the Indian border to allow the smooth entry of Bangladeshi politicians, freedom fighters and refugees was being honoured by the Indian border guards and whether the Bangladeshi leaders and their followers were being allowed to carry out their political activities in India freely and in an unfettered manner. She sounded happy when she heard both sides saying 'yes' in unison in their reply.

Indira Gandhi had lauded the role of the Bengali military and para-military men, fighting gallantly against the Pakistanis under tremendous odds. In the course of the previous month, most of them had been pushed into India and she wanted no time lost in regrouping them and turning them into a well-oiled fighting force with Indian assistance. India would do as much as it could to equip them with modern arms and equipment. She made a passing mention of the tremendous international pressure that had been brought to bear on India for supporting the just liberation war of Bangladesh.

Her second suggestion was to have in place the provisional government's administrative structure. A large number of intellectuals, besides senior and mid-level Bengali civil servants had also come over to India and pledged their support to the Mujib Nagar government. She informed Tajuddin that the West Bengal government had been told to arrange suitable space and provide other infrastructure for offices of the provisional government to start functioning in Calcutta. A spacious bungalow in Calcutta's upmarket Theatre Road area, close to the regional BSF headquarters, had been selected to serve as the office-cum-residence of the Bangladesh prime minister and his secretariat.

Her third suggestion was to send the large pool of experienced and senior Bengali diplomats as Bangladesh's own emissaries abroad to plead their country's case with foreign governments as that would carry greater credibility and conviction than Indian diplomats. If diplomatic recognition of Bangladesh had to be sought from foreign countries, Bangladesh itself would have to campaign for it internationally at various levels and world fora.

Her fourth suggestion was that the government in exile should set up a full-fledged broadcasting station in Calcutta, for which her government would provide all technical and material support. The radio would be an important tool of the Mujib Nagar government to imbue Bengalis across the border with greater nationalist spirit. It would also be a weapon for waging a psychological war against the Pakistanis. Repudiating the lies that the Pakistanis were spreading about the liberation war would be among the objectives of its broadcasts. Indira Gandhi was aware that a low-powered Bangladeshi transmitter was already operating from the jungles of Tripura, beaming its programme to Bangladesh. It could not reach its targeted listeners though because of its technical inadequacies. She wanted the set-up to be shifted to Calcutta so that the *betar kendro* (radio station) could be run professionally. With Indian support, it should be operated as a full-fledged modern radio station.

May was the month when Indian political parties, of both the left and right varieties, started taking greater interest in the happenings in East Pakistan. It must be said that among all the Indian parties, the role of the CPI was the most outstanding. Its national leaders as well as those of West Bengal were most vocal in openly and vigorously campaigning for the liberation war. Its MPs in parliament like Prof. Hiren Mukherjee, Indrajeet Gupta and Bhupesh Gupta with their matchless eloquence were forcefully espousing the cause of Bangladesh's liberation struggle on the floor of the house day after day. This lent great political weightage and support to Mrs Gandhi's policy on Bangladesh which found wide coverage in the western media. CPI's general secretary, C. Rajeswara Rao, called the Bangladesh struggle a 'national liberation movement'. This expression found mention in the party's political resolution adopted at the 9th party Congress held in Cochin that year. It was able to persuade and convince two prominent European communist parties, the French and Italian, to support its line. This they did most willingly and vociferously. The exemplary role of the firebrand Jana Sangh MP, Atal Behari Vajpayee, in supporting Mrs Gandhi's Bangladesh policy in parliament, showed that political parties, having both leftist and rightist views and inclinations, were not only united but also stood firmly behind Mrs Gandhi on the Bangladesh issue.

In contrast, the support from the CPI(M) was lukewarm because of its 'close and fraternal party-to-party ties' with China. That was a time when the Communist bloc was split into two, one led by the Soviet Communist Party (CPSU) and the other by the Chinese Communist Party (CCP), both of which were vying to provide leadership to the world communist movement. Barely a decade ago, the CPI(M) had supported China during the 1962 border skirmish, by calling India 'an aggressor' and claiming China fell prey to Indian aggression. The CPI(M) leadership knew that the CCP did not approve of the Indian involvement in the liberation struggle and played it safe initially. Many senior leaders were heard echoing Zhou Enlai's warning that under Indira Gandhi's stewardship, India would burn its fingers by getting involved in the happenings across its eastern border.

This perception changed in May when its Central Committee, seeing the entire political spectrum of India and its people standing rock solid behind Mrs Gandhi's Bangladesh policy, lent support to the liberation war by adopting a favourable resolution. Totally isolated and out of line with the current Indian mood, it desperately started correcting its course by involving its leaders and frontal organizations in various relief work for the refugees. Alongside, it also started supporting a conglomerate of seven extreme Marxist-Leninist fringe groups of Bangladesh, which had formed themselves into a Bangladesh Mukti Sangram Samannoy Committee with Maulana Bhasani as its chairman. The CPI(M) was extremely hostile to Mrs Gandhi for allowing the Awami League to dominate the liberation war effort and providing all kinds of moral and material support to it.

The other political campaign that the CPI(M) ran was to condemn Mrs Gandhi's wisdom in not granting diplomatic recognition to the provisional government forthwith; it had raised a nefarious slogan, '*Indira Yahya ek hai bhulo mat bhulo mat*' (Indira and Yahya are on the same team, don't forget, don't forget). Its Bengal leaders were heard decrying her 'partisan role' in private conversation. This, they said, amounted to stabbing the Bengali nationalist movement from behind. Worse, it also sought to overlook the internecine clashes between the Samannoy members, prompted by their serious ideological differences. These seriously undermined their credibility as a pro-liberation force. As a result, Maulana Bhasani severed his ties with the committee as he was not sure whether it supported or opposed the liberation war. Bhasani's stand on the liberation war was so uncompromising that he expelled Mashiur Rahman (Jadu Mia), general secretary of his faction of NAP, for 'hobnobbing with the Pakistanis and working against the interest of Bangladesh and trying to subvert the liberation war'. There were also four other pro-China Marxist-Leninist groups, which called themselves Purba Banglar Communist Party, led by Mohammed Toah and Abdul Haq and Matin-Alauddin, who were bitterly opposed to the Awami League's liberation war effort and did everything possible to sabotage it, including beheading of *muktijoddhas*. Two prominent pro-China left leaders belonging to the Bhasani faction of NAP, Kazi Zafar Ahmed and Rashed Khan Menon, however, came over to India and lent support to those who formed the mainstream of the liberation war.

Not only the Awami League but also the government of India became extremely wary of the role of the pro-Peking Marxist-Leninist groups coming to India. Their suspicion was that they were trying to infiltrate the rank and file of the Bangladesh freedom struggle in order to either hijack or subvert it from within. Neither the provisional government nor the Indian government had a clue about whether they had been planted by the Pakistanis and the Chinese to create serious security issues in India. What, however, was known was that those Bangladesh fringe groups had a good equation with the Indian CPI(ML) factions, leading the violent Naxalite movement in several Indian states, including West Bengal. Slogans like 'China's chairman is our chairman. China's revolutionary path is our path' were openly chanted by Indian Naxalites and also those from East Pakistan.

It was not limited to sloganeering or graffiti on the walls of towns, cities and even villages. Physical extermination of their political opponents, categorized as 'class enemies', had become their main strategy of offense. This was why Awami League leaders themselves started a thorough screening of youths at youth camps before enlisting them in the Mukti Bahini for arms training. Initially anyone with leftist leanings was turned away. He eventually went back home and joined any of the 10-12 private *bahini*s (armies) like Kader Siddiqi's Kaderia Bahini or the Hemayet Bahini, headed by a former JCO of the Pak Army, fighting the Pak military inside Bangladesh.

It was in this backdrop that the government of India gave the go-ahead for forming an exclusive Mujib Bahini, composed entirely of members of Awami League's student wing, Chhatra League, who were wedded to the ideals dear to Bangabandhu. The purpose of raising this *bahini* was to have a cadre-based political force, totally loyal to Sheikh Mujib and his ideology, to counter the emergence of any anti-liberation force, which sought to defeat the objectives of the liberation war. The other objective was to set up the 'right political infrastructure inside' so as to keep the anti-Bangladeshi forces at bay and help expedite the processes of liberation war and eventually achieve the goal of a Bengali nation. Major General Sujan Singh Uban, who had trained the Indian Army's anti-guerilla squads to fight the Naga and Mizo rebels, was put in charge of training. He had earlier trained the Indian Army's Special Frontier Force, comprising former Tibetan Khampa warriors, to fight the Chinese at the Himalayan heights. Two special camps were opened for Mujib Bahini recruits, one in Dehradun and another in neighbouring Chakrata, to impart special training in the handling of semi-automatic weapons, explosives and wireless systems.

What raised hackles in segments of the Bangladesh movement was that this *bahini* was not accountable to the Chief of the Bangladesh Forces, Col. (Retd) M.A.G. Osmani or the Bangladesh government in exile. Headed by Mujib's nephew, Sheikh Fazlul Haq Moni, its stalwarts were former leading lights of the Chhatra League like Tofael Ahmed and Abdur Rezzak, all members of a nationalist youth outfit, Bangladesh Liberation Force (BLF). The carte blanche support that this *bahini* got from Government of India's Research and Analysis Wing (RAW) soon made this outfit behave irresponsibly and in a high-handed manner inside Bangladesh. And this led to serious law-and-order problems which made its formation even more questionable. It was to checkmate the Mujib Bahini's unhealthy influence on the Bengali youths undergoing arms training in Mukti Bahini camps that both Tajuddin and advisers of Mrs Gandhi decided to remove the ban on the CPB and NAP(M) affiliated students' union members belonging to Chhatra union getting inducted into Mukti Bahini. But this decision was not liked by an influential section of the Awami League leadership which targeted Tajuddin for vicious political attacks. A group of 40 members of the party who were elected to National and Provincial assemblies appealed to the Awami League high command to immediately remove him from the post of prime minister of the provisional government in exile as well as that of the general secretary of Awami League for working against party interest. Their contention was that since Awami League formed the bulwark of the liberation war, efforts were being made to compromise its interests. Convergence of personal and political interests of both Moni and Khondokar Mushtaq made them join hands to oust Tajuddin from power. But the move failed because all those who were projected as his possible successor did not measure up to Tajuddin's stature and leadership attainments both within the party and outside. Also it was the unwavering Indian support for Tajuddin which helped in clinching the leadership issue.

Indian Muslims: Ambivalent, Antagonistic

A large section of Indian Muslims was anti-Bangladesh, to put it mildly, over those nine months of 1971. Openly or subtly, they opposed Indira Gandhi's support to the Bangladesh cause. There was only a handful of leading Bengali Muslim intellectuals including Abu Syed Ayub, Prof. Hosainur Rahman, Justice Abu Sadat Masud of the Calcutta High Court, Abdur Rezzak Khan, a CPI leader and minister in the UF Government, and Dr M.O. Ghani, a CPI legislator, who were unflinching in their support to the Bangladesh cause. Fakhruddin Ali Ahmed, then minister in Mrs Gandhi's cabinet, and a host of other Muslim Congress leaders, most notably from West Bengal, strongly opposed East Pakistan breaking away from Islamic Republic of Pakistan and emerging as a secular Bengali nationalist nation, repudiating Jinnah's two-nation theory.

Reports were also circulating in official circles that influential Muslim *jagirdar* (landed gentry) clans of Naqvis, Khans and Ahmeds of Lucknow, Oudh, Bareilly, Aligarh and Azamgarh, large chunks of whose families had migrated to West Pakistan during Partition, were repeatedly petitioning Fakhruddin Ali Ahmed and other Muslim ministers like Moinul Haq Chowdhury to stop Mrs Gandhi from supporting the Bangladesh Liberation War and breaking up Pakistan. All of them belonged to families whose members held coveted jobs in Pakistan's civil and foreign services. That they were acting at the behest of their highly placed Pakistani uncles and aunts, needed no elaboration. I distinctly recall two senior Muslim ministers, Abdus Sattar, who was number two in Siddhartha Shankar Ray's cabinet, holding the key agriculture portfolio, and Joynal Abedin, commerce and industries minister, sitting in their official chambers in Writers' Buildings (the secretariat of the West Bengal government) ranting against the Indian prime minister. I was personally present in their chambers on two different occasions to hear their harangue.

They were openly lambasting Indira Gandhi in their daily press briefings for trying to break up Pakistan. Joynal was more vociferous and abrasive, accusing Mrs Gandhi's policies of being 'patently anti-Pakistan and anti-Muslim'. He repeatedly wondered aloud where would Indian Muslims, especially, Bengalis, go and seek refuge, if East Pakistan was non-existent? He believed Indira was behaving like a Hindu Mahasabha leader, trying to dismember the only homeland created for Muslims in the world. All this would reach the ears of Chief Minister Siddhartha Shankar Ray. He took no note of them because he did not want to stoke communal passions. Both Ray's Congress government in West Bengal and the Congress government at the Centre took a principled stand of not playing up the mass killing of Hindus in East Pakistan by the Pak military or saying and doing anything that would stoke communal passion and disrupt communal peace and harmony and compromise the liberation war efforts.

There were other Muslim leaders like Joynal and Sattar in West Bengal's Opposition, those such as Syed Badruddoza of Independent Democratic Party, twice elected to Lok Sabha from Murshidabad, and Gholam Yeazdani, passport minister in the first and second United Front Government of West Bengal, who were spewing venom against Indira Gandhi, the Indian state in general and Sheikh Mujib in particular among the Muslim residents of the state bordering East Pakistan. They had to be detained for the entire period of the liberation war in the interest of national security. In fact, their campaign against the liberation war had assumed such sinister dimensions, especially in the bordering districts with large Muslim concentration, that the local administration of those areas expected a violent Muslim backlash resulting in a serious law-and-order problem. Even after the liberation of Bangladesh, they were not released and their families had to petition Sheikh Mujib to plead with the Indian prime minister for their release. Mujib sent the petition to Mrs Gandhi for her consideration. She in turn forwarded it to Siddhartha Shankar Ray, who soon released them.

The impact of their virulent campaign during those nine months had vitiated the psyche of many Bengali Muslims in the bordering districts adjoining East Pakistan. They were openly hostile to India and the newly liberated Bangladesh. Many Muslim households in Murshidabad hoisted the Pakistani flag from their housetops during those nine months on certain occasions to express their solidarity with Pakistan in its fight against the creation of Bangladesh. One instance of their terrible antipathy to the Bangladesh movement was shared by H.T. Imam, adviser to Bangladesh Prime Minister Sheikh Hasina, and the first cabinet secretary of the Mujib Nagar government who died in Dhaka in April 2021. Imam had crossed over to India with his expecting wife through the Dinajpur border soon after 25 March. She was then in an advanced stage of pregnancy and started showing early signs of labour.

With dusk fast descending, Imam's first concern was to find a safe and secure refuge for his wife. If there was an emergency, she could deliver her first baby there. He knocked on the door of the first *pucca* house that he came upon. It belonged to a well-to-do Muslim landed gentry. Opening the door, he asked: 'Where are you coming from and who are you?' Imam told him that he was a key Pak government functionary, the district magistrate of Rangamati, but had just crossed over to India responding to Sheikh Mujib's call to liberate Bangladesh. He emphasized that both he and his pregnant wife badly needed rest because of the gruelling two-day walk they had undertaken to reach India. The Muslim house owner, much to Imam and his wife's shock, shut the door on their faces saying, he could offer no refuge to those conspiring to break up Pakistan.

No amount of pleading about his wife's condition and that they would move out next morning could make the man relent. The couple met the same fate at the next two Muslim households. They finally approached a Hindu household. The head of the family told him that he had no room to spare as his house was overflowing with guests but that he had a big cowshed, where they could spend the night. 'My son was born that night in a cowshed belonging to a Hindu household amidst mooing of cows. The ladies of the family helped in the delivery in every possible way for which I am still grateful to them. I still shudder to think what would have happened had they not accommodated us in their cowshed that night. What would have happened to my wife and my firstborn?' Imam recounted this ordeal to me long after that incident just to underscore the mindset of many ordinary Bengali Muslims in West Bengal towards the Bangladesh movement.

The Bangladeshi forces, having retreated into Indian territory in the face of unremitting onslaught of the Pak military, were busy regrouping, reorganizing and turning themselves into regular military formations like battalions and brigades. The Indian military officers were busy training the young Bengali recruits for the Mukti Bahini in the especially set up training camps in Uttar Pradesh, Arunachal Pradesh, Bihar, West Bengal, Assam, Mizoram and elsewhere. Senior major generals like S.S. Uban and Shahbeg Singh and six brigadiers had been put in charge of their training. Prime Minister Tajuddin Ahmed, wearing a Mao-like cap, regularly visited the training and the youth camps to keep up the morale of the *bahini* volunteers. Three brigades comprising eight infantry battalions and three artillery batteries came into being under the leadership of Major Ziaur Rahman, Maj. Khaled Mosharraf and Maj. K.M. Shafiullah. Besides, sector commanders were appointed to carry out military operations in 11 sectors of the country. The three brigades, composed wholly of regular soldiers numbering 30,000 men, who had defected from the Pak military, were called the 'Niyomito Bahini' (regular force) and the volunteers who had joined the Mukti Bahini were called 'Gano Bahini' (people's force), which was especially trained in hit-and-run guerilla warfare and use of explosives to destroy East Pakistan's economic assets like bridges, power installations and road network.

Col. Osmani, Majors Shafiullah and Khaled Mosharraf prepared the historic Teliapara document, a strategy blueprint to be followed by the trained Mukti Bahini volunteers for their operations inside East Pakistan. Its sole purpose was to keep the Pak military perpetually on the edge. The other objective was to bleed it continually. The document became the operation manual of the Mukti Bahini and it was like a bible for the *bahini*. It provided the strategy for carrying out hit-and-run raids against the Pak military posts and convoys, disrupting its line of communication and physically eliminating collaborators and *razakar*s raised and supported by the Pak military to fight as their auxiliary forces. The document was crucial as batches of trained Mukti Bahini volunteers, after completing their training, were being readied along the border to infiltrate into Bangladesh in small groups of fives and 10s for guerilla operations. For this purpose, India had already begun to arm them with semi-automatic weapons like Israeli Sten guns, self-loading rifles (SLRs), grenades and mortars.

Shahbeg and Sant Singh

One of the least known facets behind the Mukti Bahini's emergence as a dreaded guerilla force happens to be the excellent rapport that the likes of Major General Shahbeg Singh and Brigadier Sant Singh were able to establish with the recruits. They were among a dozen senior officers of the Indian Army, entrusted with the task of raising and training the freedom fighters. The personal chemistry between the teachers and their students was of such high quality that it engendered a deep sense of commitment towards the liberation war. It evoked admiration even among those whose dislike for the Indian Army was well known. They lived with the recruits in their tents, shared their spartan and frugal meals and learnt Bengali to communicate with them in their mother tongue. They also loved sharing their dreams as evolving warriors. All this developed into a close and emotional bonding between the two and the recruits were willing to carry out the orders of their 'Sirs' in letter and spirit even at the cost of their lives.

Major General Shahbeg Singh, for instance, got so emotionally involved in training the recruits that he did not take a day's leave nor was he in touch with his family in Punjab for a year. He never left the training camp in Agartala. So strong was his 'total commitment' to imparting training to 'my boys' (a term he used fondly when referring to the *bahini* volunteers), that the only letter he wrote in a year was to his wife in early December 1971 informing her in one line 'I am OK', the letter carrying his pseudonym signature 'Shah Baig'. The letter carried the bogus address of an Agartala shopkeeper so that his wife could not reply. He even did away with the main symbol of his Sikh pride and identity, by cutting his *kesh* (hair) and quitting his turban so that the recruits could consider him as 'one of their very own'. To them he became a father figure and he called them by their first names. To the trainees, he became a living legend. This devotion to training turned the raw Mukti Bahini recruits into intrepid, daredevil guerillas. Seeing his excellent rapport with the recruits, Lt Gen. Jagjit Singh Aurora, GOC-in-C, Indian Eastern Command, made Shahbeg in charge of Mukti Bahini's Delta sector in Agartala, responsible for planning, organizing and directing guerilla operations in eastern and central Bangladesh. In close cooperation and co-ordination with Major Khaled Mosharraf, commander of sector II, and also of the K Brigade, he executed the daring guerilla strike on Dacca's heavily fortified Inter-Continental Hotel on 9 June, where a visiting World Bank team was staying, with handpicked Mukti Bahini commandos. The operation was done in a car hijacked from Gulshan, an upmarket residential area of Dacca, after breaching the hotel's security ring. Six hand grenades were lobbed at or around the revolving door of the hotel when the World Bank team was about to enter the hotel lobby. Power stations in Dacca and around were targeted and put out of commission in hand-grenade attacks. The Pak Army suffered sizable casualties in this first-ever guerilla strike on Dacca.

The attack was meant to disprove the tall Pakistani claim that the situation and life in Dacca was 'absolutely normal' and was 'wholly under Government's control'. When Shahbeg died in operation 'Blue Star' inside the Golden Temple, the first to inform me about it was his former Mukti Bahini trainee. He rang me up from Dhaka early in the morning after hearing the BBC radio broadcast that his 'respected Sir was no more'. Subsequently many of his other trainees rang me up to condole the 'sad, tragic ending of a gallant, loving teacher and Sir'. And yet such unkind and uncalled-for comments were made about Shahbeg and Uban's capabilities as guerilla warfare teachers by some officers of the Niyomito Bahini that I had begun to wonder the purpose of running them down in the presence of Mukti Bahini recruits. My take was that it was deliberately done to humiliate them so that seeds of disharmony and disrespect could be sown in the minds of impressionable recruits towards their 'Sirs'. Comments like: 'The Indian Army officers belong to a soft and ceremonial army good at performing only ceremonial drills and march past but not good at imparting guerilla training like the famous Vietnamese general Vo Nguyen Giap or Fidel Castro's right-hand comrade the legendary Cuban revolutionary Che Guevera.' They even questioned the wisdom of the provisional government in allowing officers like Uban and Shahbeg impart arms and guerilla warfare training to *mukti* and Mujib Bahini recruits as their track record of imparting such training to men of the Indian Army was 'very dismal'.

The reason for this bitterness, *I discovered,* stemmed from the complaints of Col. (Retd) Osmani and other key functionaries of the Bangladesh government who were hurt by the 'overbearing attitude' of their Indian counterpart like D.P. Dhar, P.N. Haksar, Lt General Jagjit Singh Aurora and Lt General J.F.R. Jacob. According to Osmani, D.P. Dhar never kept his scheduled appointments with him and on most occasions kept him waiting for more than an hour in the waiting room along with other visitors. Osmani being highly exacting in keeping time and appointments felt extremely slighted every time he was kept waiting in D.P. Dhar's waiting room or ante chamber along with other visitors waiting to see him. The complaint against Aurora and Jacob was that they seldom treated Osmani with enough respect. Both of them were very conscious of their superior rank and behaved indifferently with him. Osmani had once narrated his bitterness about Dhar's 'cold and careless' attitude towards him in a tête-à-tête with me after the liberation.

From mid-June onwards India's involvement in the liberation struggle became more pronounced and it started equipping the Mukti Bahini with automatic weapons to inflict greater damage to the Pak military. About 2,000 Mukti Bahini guerillas who had received training in various Indian camps started infiltrating deep inside Bangladesh to carry out daring raids on Pak military positions. They infiltrated under the cover of heavy pounding of Pak border outposts by the Indian artillery. Simultaneously, casualties mounted and the *mukti*s especially those seriously injured were brought to India and treated at Indian military hospitals. This sudden change in the stance of *mukti*s mounting frequent attacks on Pak positions followed publication of alarming reports of two foreign study groups. One was by the World Bank and the other by Oxfam. The first one was invited and commissioned by Yahya himself, to study the food and economic situation in East Pakistan so as to assess and recommend what should be the quantum of aid, both financial and food, to be given to Pakistan by the World Bank and other international aid agencies to tide over an impending economic crisis. Yahya was forced to undertake this exercise as economically Pakistan was in dire straits since the western donors of Aid Pakistan Consortium at its meeting in Paris in April had refused to make a definitive aid pledge amount and announced suspension of aid for one year because of the political upheaval that had overtaken East Pakistan. Both the groups had predicted prevalence of famine-like conditions and a steep economic downturn overtaking the eastern province in the coming months.

The reports forewarned that food shortage and continuing violence would further exacerbate the refugee influx into India. This meant that there was a distinct possibility of another several million refugees streaming into India unhindered, in search of food, shelter and livelihood in the latter part of 1971. This was because all agricultural and economic activity had come to a halt due to the political turmoil in the province. These reports created such a scare in Delhi's official circle that Mrs Gandhi and her advisers started getting nightmares. This was told to me by Sukhomoy Chakravarty, then a member of the Planning Commission. Mrs Gandhi and her advisers realized that a war was absolutely necessary to stop further exodus of refugees if India was to be saved from a certain catastrophe. Already their office desks were piled up with intelligence reports and letters appealing for help from the chief ministers of the bordering states who complained that the refugee crisis had led to serious deterioration in the law-and-order situation in their respective territories.

Given the overcrowding and squalor in camps, the refugees were coming out in large numbers and mingling with the local population in search of jobs. This had given rise to tension and even led to clashes between them and the locals. The chief ministers had warned that if the refugee exodus was not immediately checked, the situation in the bordering states would go out of the government's control and total anarchy (in the form of communal riots fomented by Pakistani agents) would prevail in highly sensitive border areas. Delhi got further confirmation of Yahya's sinister designs against India from the senior Pakistani diplomat of Bengali origin, Humayun Rashid Chaudhuri, who had just defected from the Pakistan High Commission in Delhi. He warned Delhi that the Pak president was preparing his government and the military to 'punish India further'. General Yahya wanted to overwhelm India with a bigger refugee crisis and riots so that its resources and energy would be wholly consumed in managing this apocalypse-like situation.

India countered by stepping up its role and involvement in the liberation war. It began training the Bangladeshi naval commandos at

Plassey on the river Bhagirathi by its own naval specialists for waging underwater warfare. The objective was to detonate Pakistani vessels with explosives in the two main seaports, Chittagong and Chalna, so that East Pakistan's tenuous sea link with West Pakistan could be severely disrupted. Seven Bengali submariners of the Pakistan navy, who had defected in France, provided the nucleus of this commando force. Its strength eventually rose to almost 500 and it played havoc from July-August onwards, in sinking numerous Pakistani merchant and naval vessels at these two major seaports, which until November, were clogged with about 51,000 tons of sunken vessels. This forced foreign and Pakistani ships to stay away from them. Inland vessels carrying supplies for the military and operating in two major riverine ports at Chandpur and Narayanganj were also targeted and almost put out of operation. As a result, the Pak military's Eastern Command's supply chain was badly hit, disrupting its essential bulk of military supplies from West Pakistan and compromising its operational capability.

The heroic exploits of the Bengali naval commandos form a glorious saga in the history of Bangladesh Liberation War. Unfortunately, much of their contribution to the liberation war effort remained unknown for a long time. The role of Indian naval officers, especially its frogmen, in raising and training the highly specialized underwater demolition squads in a matter of weeks has, sadly, remained unknown and unacknowledged. Many of them volunteered to accompany the trainees on dangerous missions and in the process almost lost their life and limbs. Interestingly most of the Bengali youths who wanted to be frogmen came from the peasant stock with little or no formal education. It was the prowess of their character and grit and determination to be part of this elite commando force of the Mukti Bahini which ensured their recruitment into this highly specialized committed group of freedom fighters who mastered the complicated skills of underwater demolition in the shortest possible time. In the process many got killed while undergoing hands-on training. But this did not in any way dim their craze and resolve for joining this force.

A nucleus of Bangladesh Air Force (BAF) was later formed in Dimapur in Nagaland in August-September with the help of the Bengali officers who had defected from Pakistan. The air force was led by Air Cmmdr A.K. Khondokar and Group Captain Sultan Mahmud. The Bengali civilian pilots of the PIA were also inducted into the newly formed BAF, which was provided with a Dakota, an Otter and two Alouette helicopters by the Indian Air Force for training and operation. In November, it carried out daring air raids code-named 'Operation Kilo Flight' by dropping bombs on oil depots of the Chittagong oil refinery and also at Narayanganj river port from an Otter, whose compass and radio malfunctioned throughout the flight operation. The two raids starved the Pak military of much needed oil supplies, thereby severely restricting their movements during the November-December period at the height of the liberation war.

I had visited two Mukti Bahini training camps in Raiganj, West Dinajpur in West Bengal and Chakulia in Bihar, where the Indian Army's junior and non-commissioned (JCOs and NCOs) officers were making the raw recruits, mostly from peasant backgrounds, go through the paces of military training; doing field drill, exercises, handling weapons and ambushing enemy patrols. I was amazed by the ability of the recruits to adapt themselves to the demands and challenges of their new roles as freedom fighters that the liberation war had offered them. The Indian military instructors were fulsome in their praise for the alacrity with which they had learnt the ropes of weapons handling, laying mines and ambushing enemy patrols within a fortnight. Peasants who had only known the art of handling the ploughshare in fields for growing crops had now mastered the art of firing mortar shells, semi-automatic guns and detonating powerful explosives to destroy bridges and culverts with ease.

Recruits who had never heard and spoken anything but Bengali in their lives understood their instructors' Hindi commands without much difficulty. What transformed each one of them almost overnight from ordinary farmers to committed freedom fighters was their irrepressible urge to take on the *Khan Sena* headlong in battles at the earliest. They wanted to prove that they were no less than the *Khan Sena* in fighting capabilities. This singular motivation helped swell the rank and file of freedom fighters and drove them to perform heroics, which surprised and shocked even the Pakistani establishment. They wanted to disprove the boastful remark of the Pak army chief, General Hamid Khan, that 'coward Bengalis will be on the run even before the military fired the first shot'. Hamid Khan's slanderous racial comment and other racial slurs heaped upon the Bengalis by other leading Pakistanis, became the prime catalyst in motivating the ordinary village folks to take up arms against the Pakistanis.

During my stay in Raiganj, I heard murmurs of protest from another group of visiting Niyomito Bahini officers who were 'dead against' Indian Army personnel training Bangladeshi recruits. They said, 'We want Made in Bangladesh and not Made in India Mukti Bahini recruits.' They would also accuse the Indian military of indoctrinating the minds of young impressionable freedom fighters with Indian ethos and stances. According to them, India was doing this with the long-term end of creating a constituency of its own and an influential interest group, which could be manoeuvred in Bangladesh to suit its political needs in future. This charge was wholly unfounded and malicious because none of the instructors did anything else except provide arms and drill training in those camps. I had personally attended the training sessions of the recruits, where the instructors never preached anything political in nature or anything at all that could remotely be construed as peddling any political line or even extolling India's help in the liberation war.

What surprised me was the way those officers gave vent to their feelings quite openly and bitterly. I had countered them by asking: 'Why are you not getting involved in training the Mukti Bahini?' The answers were quite contradictory and made little sense. 'We don't have the time and the wherewithal to do this. But if we do, who would be leading the Mukti Bahini's fight against the Pakistanis?' Significantly, one of the four officers who were questioning India's 'ulterior motive' in training the Mukti Bahini, joined President Ziaur Rahman's newly floated Bangladesh Nationalist Party (BNP)-led government in 1978 after Bangabandhu's assassination and was inducted as a minister into Zia's cabinet. Some others were recruited as ministers in Hussain Muhammed Ershad's government.

When I brought these comments to the notice of the provisional government leaders, they were visibly embarrassed but they made light of the issue by saying those young officers were yet to free themselves from the hangover of the Pak military tradition and training that was anti-India centric. Since they had been reared in the Pakistani military tradition, which perceived India as its 'treacherous enemy', this mindset was not unusual, explained A.H.M. Qamaruzzaman, Bangladesh's home minister, to me.

Meanwhile Mrs Gandhi's stalling an Indian military intervention in Bangladesh and granting recognition to the provisional government was causing misgivings among a section of the officers of Niyomito Bahini and some ministers and officials of the Mujib Nagar government. They used it as a plea to spread disaffection and also to lower the morale of the rank and file of the Bangladesh political elements, who had sought refuge in India to wage the liberation war. The idea was to rally support among the Bangladesh group against the Indian leadership and also question the Indian Army's capability to take on the Pak military by spreading canards against it. The ultimate objective was to undermine Bangabandhu's dream and vision for achieving Bengali nationhood and also subverting the spadework done by him in this direction for decades.

Although the acting president, Syed Nazrul Islam, and the prime minister, Tajuddin Ahmed, appreciated Mrs Gandhi's compulsion in not granting their 'twin wishes', they never questioned the intentions of the Indian leadership nor did they say or do anything to run down the image of the Indian Army. On the contrary, they always praised Mrs Gandhi and her government for doing 'unthinkable things for Bangladesh'. The Mushtaq coterie and some others started saying that the Indian Army was 'not equal to Pak Army and was scared of the might of the Pakistan Army'. Oxford-based noted Indian writer Nirad C. Chaudhuri endorsed this view in an article published in a London daily and said that Indian journalists' reports on East Pakistan suffered from a serious credibility gap. This further reinforced the Mushtaq clique's view that India wanted to avoid a military confrontation at any cost. During my stay with Ziaur Rahman at his Tura camp in August, he, in my presence, had berated the 'fighting capabilities and qualities' of the Indian Army saying that, in the 1965 war, he had personally experienced it while successfully repulsing 'feeble, unplanned and poorly executed' Indian attacks in the Punjab sector.

This coterie had also begun to question the Indian leadership's political will to take on Pakistan and it continued to pose mischievously loaded questions to fan anti-India sentiment among the Bangladesh political elements and intellectuals living in India.

The arguments were vicious. 'Was it in India's national interest to go to war with Pakistan on the Bangladesh issue and incur forbidding costs? The only motive that could spur India into action would be to send the refugees back home. What else does India gain by embarking on war against Pakistan? So, it is wrong on our part to expect India to fight for us which it could have easily done immediately after the crackdown. But it didn't. Moreover, it is no economic and military power of any consequence. Whether it can sustain itself by materially supporting the Mukti Bahini for the next six months is now a moot question. India has made a fool of us by giving the impression that it will.' They even asked whether the Indira government was using the refugee influx to hoodwink the Indian people and cover up its 'gross failures' on the economic and political fronts. They also wondered whether her government was using the refugee issue as a means to get more foreign aid from donors to 'revitalize its sick and collapsing economy'. A Bangladeshi journal, *Aagami*, run by Khondokar Mushtaq, edited and published from Calcutta with the help of some leading Bengali intellectuals living in the city, even gave a call for a 'violent movement against the Indira government', to expose her government's 'perfidious act in befooling the Bengalis'.

'Why Mujib and our present leadership are looking toward a Hindu India for help in breaking up an Islamic country is a big mystery,' opined *Aagami*. This subtle and crafty anti-India and anti-Mujib campaign continued for weeks. This rhetoric did succeed in influencing many negatively; even a fully committed and enlightened freedom fighter like Nurul Kader Khan, then the secretary of one of the key administrative divisions of the Mujib Nagar government and a close confidant of Prime Minister Tajuddin Ahmed. He was visibly worried by this campaign. Taken in by this deceitful propaganda, he expressed his frustration to me in early June about the 'liberation war not heading anywhere' especially after the announcement of Mrs Gandhi's no-intervention decision. The prospect of the emergence of an independent Bangladesh anytime soon, looked 'very bleak' not only to this 'mischievous lobby' but also to others, himself included.

This lobby painted such a gloomy and defeatist scenario about the liberation war that it had begun to drive hordes of freedom fighters to despair and hopelessness. Sitting in his Southern Avenue office, Nurul Kader gave vent to his dismay over the wily campaign being carried out by this influential coterie whose thrust was that since 'nothing tangible' had been achieved in the last three-and-a-half months by resisting the Pak military, except suffering the loss of countless innocent and valuable lives, it was high time to introspect and return home and work out a settlement with the Pak military within the Pakistani framework. This negative perception started gaining further ground after an influential Awami League leader Mizanur Rahman Chowdhury at a closed-door meeting of his party's 300 elected MNAs and MPAs held in early July in Siliguri said that with India giving bogus and unconvincing reasons for denying recognition to Bangladesh, besides going back on its promise to provide adequate supplies of arms and ammunition for the freedom fighters, its credibility as Bangladesh's well-wisher had suffered badly. It could no longer be trusted. 'Naturally we have begun to seriously doubt whether it will ever fully support our war of liberation when its final phase eventually begins. In such a gloomy scenario it is much better to go back home and continue our struggle with our own resources or reach a compromise with the Pakistani generals.' He concluded his speech by demanding Tajuddin's resignation as the head of the Bangladesh government as he had failed to strategize and lead the liberation war along the right line.

But Tajuddin gave such a thundering and well-argued retort, defending India's stand on Bangladesh, that the gathering heard him spellbound, and when he finished his speech, he got a standing ovation amid deafening chants of '*Joy Bangla* and *Joy Bangabandhu*'. My MNA and MPA friends who were present at that meeting told me that Khondokar Mushtaq had manipulated Mizanur, who was not his camp follower, to target Tajuddin and India so as to unsettle the freedom movement and force it to go on the backfoot. Nurul Kader himself had begun to wonder whether he had done the right thing by coming to India to continue waging the liberation war. What was also being talked about by this coterie was that the provincial governor Lieutenant General Tikka Khan had brought life in East Pakistan almost back to normal with trains and flights operating on schedule, government and commercial offices open, and banks transacting their normal business.While Khondokar Mushtaq tried to mess up the political leadership, Ziaur Rahman about the same time tried to do something similar by upsetting and disturbing the military set-up that had already come into existence and gradually started functioning. He along with the support of half-a-dozen young sector commanders wanted Col. (Retd) M.A.G. Osmani's removal from the post of chief of the armed forces as he was unable to inspire and successfully lead the Mukti Bahini in its military operation. He wanted Osmani to be 'kicked upstairs' as the defence minister of the provisional government. He was for the setting up of a 'war council' that he would head and have five to six young sector commanders of proven ability to direct the Mukti Bahini's operations. Osmani felt so humiliated that he tendered his resignation but Tajuddin refused to accept it as that, he feared, would badly dent the morale and thoroughly disorient the entire Mukti Bahini in taking on the Pak military. Because of these disturbing developments the Indian political and military leadership were not able to correctly read and gauge the mind of the Bangladeshi political leaders and their military commanders. For quite some time this threw a spanner in the works of the plans and programmes that the Indian leadership had drawn up for Mukti Bahini. As Khondokar was unable to score politically against Tajuddin he chose devious paths to subvert the freedom movement. He entrusted his trusted bureaucrat and lieutenant, the foreign secretary of the provisional government, Nazrul Islam 'Chashi', with the task of conceptualizing and propagating the idea of Bangladesh having a loose confederation with Pakistan 'for avoiding further bloodshed'. According to declassified Congressional records, at least seven to eight meetings were held between Khondokar's trusted MNAs and Mr Griffin, the American consul general, inside the American consulate in Calcutta between August and September. According to Saradindu Chattopadhyay of BSF's intelligence wing, Khondokar had also held one meeting in the hotel suite of a senior State Department official who had specially flown in from Washington for this purpose. As the declassified documents reveal, the American ambassador in Islamabad John Farland was asked by Henry Kissinger, national security adviser to President Nixon, to approach President Yahya with the proposal to start negotiating with elements of the Bangladesh government in Calcutta. Yahya had accepted the proposal much against his wishes because he was against holding discussions with any renegade elements of his country. The reason for the Nixon administration to take such extraordinary interest in Bangladesh's affairs was because it considered Pakistan 'a bulwark for sub-continental stability for which it had to be preserved on the Islamic basis at any cost' (Declassified Congressional records). The upshot of those secret meetings was that Khondokar promised to both the Americans and Pakistanis that he as the foreign minister of Bangladesh during his proposed trip to New York in late September as the head of the Bangladesh delegation to the UN would announce a compromise formula whose focus would be not to snap all the linkages of the eastern province with that of its western unit but retain some of them so that Bangladesh continued to be a part of Islamic Republic of Pakistan. This would deny it the status of a full-fledged independent nation. In other words, it would rescind at one go all the decisions and actions that Mujib had taken over decades to realize his long-cherished dream of turning East Pakistan into an independent Bengali nation. Also it would bring to naught all the untold suffering that Mujib and others had undergone and the sacrifices they had made for achieving their goal. Besides it would bring down the curtain on the liberation war that the provisional government was waging from Indian soil. Both Tajuddin and the Indian government came to know about his treacherous move and divested him of his responsibility of leading the Bangladesh delegation to New York. But Khondokar remained defiant.

A Sinister Campaign

Not to be outdone, Khondokar and his lobby launched a vicious, sinister and divisive campaign. To confuse, demotivate and disorient the freedom fighters about the objectives of the liberation war, Khondokar had begun to visit the Mukti Bahini camps and mischievously ask the trainees: 'Do you know why are you taking arms training? Is it for achieving Bangladesh's independence or securing Mujib's release from prison?' To confuse them further, he would say: 'You cannot have both at one go. It is either or. If you want independence, you will not get Sheikh Mujib alive.' Most of the trainees were so befuddled by these posers that they approached their Indian military trainers, known as *ustads* (experts) for answers. They advised them to consult their political leaders for guidance. The provisional government's view was that Khondokar was mischievously parroting the conditions that either the Pakistanis or the Americans had laid down for Mujib's release or Bangladesh's independence while holding negotiations with him.

Khondokar had also objected to the presence of a poster series in the tents where the trainees lived. It showed gun-wielding Muslim, Hindu and Buddhist freedom fighters against the backdrop of their places of worship fighting the war of liberation together as Bengalis. The secular content of the posters had offended Khondokar so much that he told the freedom fighters without any hesitation, 'Since most of you are Muslims, for Allah's sake don't practise secularism. *Shudhu Allah Allah karo*' (Take only the almighty Allah's name).

It was to counter this political mischief by Khondokar Mushtaq that Prime Minister Tajuddin Ahmed began to visit both the Mukti Bahini and the youth camps at frequent intervals. He addressed the recruits to provide them with the right answers. I was at one such meeting held at the Mukti Bahini headquarters in Kalyani, where he provided them with the 'correct perspective'. He said his government was trying to achieve both the objectives together. Victory in the liberation war will ensure Bangabandhu's automatic release; unharmed. One could not be had without the other. Bengalis would have to achieve both simultaneously. And that day was not very far when they would be achieving both the objectives together,' said Tajuddin amidst thunderous applause from the trainee freedom fighters. He emphasized that as Bengalis, belonging to different creeds, they were fighting their *muktijuddho* as one. He ended by saying he was confident that he had been able to clear the misgivings and confusion created in their minds by some about the objectives of the liberation war. He reiterated that Bangabandhu's release from Pakistani prison was their topmost priority, as also securing the independence of 75 million Bengalis. Never once did he mention the names of Khondokar Mushtaq and his camp followers or say anything ill of them even indirectly. These points became the refrain of his subsequent speeches. At every such meeting, his unmatched patriotic fervour and unflinching loyalty to Sheikh Mujib were there for everyone to see and realize his total commitment to the twin objectives.

At Kalyani, however, he made oblique references to attempts being made by some of his colleagues to portray him 'as power hungry and ambitious'. He explained that throughout his life he had never run after positions of power and authority. Bangabandhu, in the presence of those same colleagues, had assigned him the task of leading the liberation war in his absence in clear and in unambiguous terms. He further said he had never asked Bangabandhu to place this onerous responsibility on him. As the prime minister of the provisional government, he was just carrying out Bangabandhu's instruction to the best of his ability. The main focus of his work during the last few months, he said, had been to realize his dream of establishing an independent Bengali nation. Achieving this goal and securing Bangabandhu's release were now his 'only sacred *sadhana* [mission] in life'. During the entire period of the liberation war, he led the life of an ascetic at his office-cum-residence in the Theatre Road bungalow. He cut himself off totally from his family, never bothering to meet his wife and children or maintaining any line of communication with them. It was at Kalyani that I first learnt that his leadership was being seriously challenged from within the party, though I was fully aware of his strained relation with Khondokar Mushtaq, Sheikh Fazlul Haq Moni and their camp followers.

The buzzword in Awami circles during those days was that Mushtaq was trying to manipulate mid-level and senior Awami League leaders into revolting against Tajuddin, and was egging them on to undermine his leadership. Having realized that the country's liberation was round the corner, they did not want him to continue as the prime minister as they themselves had become too ambitious for power and had their own agenda, both personal and political, to fulfil. On the slightest pretext they would hurl unseemly invectives at him and his confidants even in the presence of Indian media men and officials. I was witness to many such incidents one of which I will recount here. After the Garibpur drubbing the Pakistani brigade in Jessore panicked and started pulling back its men from the Jessore–Khulna border with India. The small border town of Debhata on the banks of the Kalindi river was the place from where the first pullout took place soon after the Garibpur battle in the third week of November. News about this reached the government in exile in Calcutta and Tajuddin Ahmed immediately assigned his trusted lieutenant Barrister Amirul Islam and some other senior Awami League leaders including K.M. Obaidur Rahman besides the sector commander of the region Major Jalil to make an on-the-spot visit. The dashing Indian sub-divisional officer of Basirhat Y.V. Saptarshi, IAS, was also included as part of the study team to look into the administrative requirements because of an administrative vaccum that existed in the area. Reports were coming in that pro-Pakistani elements in the towns and surrounding villages were persecuting households whose members had joined the Mukti Bahini and were extorting money from them. Tajuddin wanted the writ of the government in exile not only to run but also reign supreme in areas from where the Pakistanis were pulling out. He did not want any power vacuum to exist in those areas. We all travelled in a station wagon upto Itindaghat and from there boarded a launch for Debhata. Barrister Amirul Islam sat comfortably in the front seat while we squeezed ourselves into the rear seats of the five-seater vehicle. When we boarded the launch, a special chair was placed on the deck for Barrister Islam to sit on. This enraged Obaidur Rahman no end. He could not suppress his irritation and gave vent to his anger. 'I have been badly humiliated by this stooge of Tajuddin and tolerated enough insults. Despite being a senior leader of the Awami League and hailing from Faridpur I am being treated as riff-raff. The country is not free yet and these stooges of Tajuddin think that they have become VVIPs. No wonder so many people in the party are rallying round Khondokar Mushtaq. I will go and complain to him when we get back to Calcutta.' Barrister Islam kept his cool and did not answer back. But there was no stopping Obaidur Rahman. 'I know why this is being done and at whose behest. Because I do not acknowledge

Tajuddin as my leader,' he thundered. Fearing Obaid's outburst might take a nasty turn, Major Jalil intervened. 'There are Indian friends around. *Allahr wastey chup karen.*' But by then a big local crowd had collected and was witness to this unseemly episode which laid bare the deep fissure that was fast developing inside the Awami League leadership. I could at once feel what kind of challenges Tajuddin was facing against his leadership inside the party.

Nurul Kader had also narrated an interesting conversation that a reputed columnist of a leading Dacca Bengali daily had with the news editor of an English Dacca daily, both of whom met perchance in central Dacca's leading shopping complex in early May. The columnist told the journalist that he and his family had completed arrangements to go to India's Tripura to take part in the liberation war just as many of his friends and acquaintances had already done in recent weeks. The journalist questioned the columnist's wisdom of going to India as the Pak military had already been successful in breaking the back of the Bengali resistance movement and was in the process of restoring normalcy in the province fast. The purpose of narrating the story was to underscore the changing perception of Dacca's elite about the fate of the liberation war, though this senior journalist subsequently came to Calcutta whose purpose was shrouded in mystery. Because he went back to East Pakistan as surreptitiously as he had come to the city.

The prevailing sense of despondency affected many others, unsure about the course that the liberation war would take. They asked whether it was the right time to return home or get stuck in India for an indefinite period and bear the interminable suffering stoically. Indira Gandhi's proximity to the Soviet Union and seeking its support on Bangladesh was also disliked in the provisional government circles. But not by Tajuddin and Nazrul Islam. The Soviets were perceived as 'no match for Americans' as a world power as they were 'lacking in resources'. They underscored the point time and again that if Pakistan and America teamed up with China against India, Delhi would find itself hopelessly outmatched, outclassed and outmanoeuvred diplomatically, militarily and politically on the Bangladesh issue. What added to the worries of the Mujib Nagar government was that both the US and Chinese governments, out of their own self-interest, had decided to arm Yahya's military against India and the Mukti Bahini. According to Warren Unna's reports appearing in *The Statesman* between late November and early December 1971, President Nixon even ignored the Congressional restrictions on supplying arms to Pakistan as he felt a 'Soviet stooge' like India should not be allowed to humiliate its long-standing ally, Pakistan, and overrun its eastern province.

Meanwhile, reports were appearing in the Indian print media that senior officials in the Nixon administration did not approve of the president's pronounced tilt towards Pakistan. Some of them were leaking sensitive documents, including the gist of cables sent by American envoys based in Delhi and Dacca, to the well-known syndicated American columnist Jack Anderson. Based on those documents, Anderson was writing blistering syndicated columns against the Nixon administration in highly rated and widely read American dailies and journals. That the US envoy in India, Kenneth Keating, in his dispatches to Washington had urged President Nixon to 'adopt a more positive policy toward India' in view of the 'very serious refugee problem that India was facing' also got mentioned in one of Anderson's incisive pieces. Keating, being a political appointee of Nixon, was hopeful that the president would pay heed to his recommendation and do a course correction. He had even written to the president that: 'India being the world's most populous democracy more than ever needed American help and backing' (US National Security Archive and Declassified State Department documents). He predicted that if Pakistan continued with its policy of using military force as a means for resolving East Pakistan's political problem, it would 'inevitably lead to the break-up of the country'. In one of his notable pieces, Anderson ascribed President Nixon's pro-Pakistan tilt to his 'rabid anti-Indian' outlook.

Soon after the crackdown of 25 March, Keating had strongly emphasized the need for the president to make a statement against Pakistan. He wanted the US government to publicly deplore Pakistani brutality. He felt appalled that the Pakistanis had committed atrocities with American arms. He wanted a political solution. But Nixon was against a political solution as that would amount to letting down one of his most trusted allies in Asia. Instead he called Keating a 'traitor' for taking a pronounced pro-India stand and Kissinger said Keating had been taken over by the Indians. *The Statesman*'s legendary Washington correspondent Warren Unna reported much of the content of the leaked documents appearing in the US print media in both the Calcutta and Delhi editions of *The Statesman*. Unna's grand exposé of Nixon's Pakistan and Bangladesh policy had put him on top of the 'master list' of the US president's detractors. So sharp and biting was his reportage that Henry Kissinger considered him, like Jack Anderson, Nixon's 'personal enemy'. That the US consul general in Dacca, Archer Blood, who strongly disapproved of the Nixon administration's Pakistan policy was sending 'incendiary and rhetoric filled telegrams' to the State Department, on the prevailing situation in East Pakistan, also got leaked in the US media. Besides, leading senators of the Democratic Party like Ted Kennedy and Frank Church were keeping up the barrage of criticism of Nixon for not restraining Pakistan from pursuing its policy of bloody repression. These reports were also splashed in the Indian media. Such encouraging news brought some comfort and lifted the spirits of both the Indian and Bangladeshi leaders, who started seeing a faint light at the long end of their tunnel of distress and delay.

The untamed Pakistani president, however, went ahead with further strengthening his Dacca-based Eastern Command. By late May he had airlifted two fully equipped battle-hardened infantry divisions from West Pakistan, which had emboldened his military commanders in the east to be more aggressive. Many Mukti Bahini camps along the border and Indian civilian targets had been pounded with mortar and artillery shells in Tripura and West Bengal resulting in heavy casualties. Yahya was in no mood for giving in politically as he got the Pakistan Election Commission to hold a farcical by-election for 'vacant seats' of Awami League MNAs and MPAs, who had sought refuge in India. The Pak Election Commission had already declared those seats 'vacant' and the by-elections were held without any contest. Besides, the Jamaat e Islami leaders of East Pakistan were urging Yahya to annex north Bengal and Assam by invading India's strategic weak point – the Chicken's Neck or the Siliguri corridor. This made Indira Gandhi hand over the charge of border security and protection to the army. The BSF was ill-equipped to meet the Pakistani military challenge. Indian military camps and fortifications came up all along the border, serving as a deterrent to any Pakistani military misadventure.

At a time when the morale of the Mujib Nagar government functionaries was at its lowest ebb, disturbing news started reaching both Delhi and Calcutta that American envoys and other senior diplomats in various East European capitals had held secret parleys with their Chinese counterparts. The agenda of their discussion was not known. Soviet diplomats, who had kept close tabs on Sino-US diplomatic engagement, felt that the Chinese, suffering from a sense of insecurity, especially after the Ussuri face-off and invasion of Czechoslovakia, were extremely worried about the Soviet Union launching a full-scale attack against China any day, and were keen on courting their arch enemy, the Americans, as their strategic partner.

Encouraged by the positive Chinese vibes and extremely worried by the growing Soviet influence in Asia, Nixon wanted a more meaningful and direct engagement with the highest Chinese leadership to rein in the political and military ambitions of the Soviets in Asia. He wanted China to be the counterbalance to the Soviets in Asia and was looking for a facilitator, who enjoyed the full confidence of the Chinese leadership, to act as the go-between among the leaders of the two countries. He would also have to be one who could keep the secret diplomatic engagement under the strictest wrap. Neither the Americans nor the Chinese wanted to lose face by making diplomatic overtures without being sure that the other side would respond positively.

In July 1969, when President Nixon visited Pakistan, he told Yahya that he would highly appreciate it, if the Pakistani president, whose proximity to the CCP leadership was well known, would convey to Peking his offer of reaching 'wide-ranging accommodation' and 'building an enduring relationship' with China. For this he wanted his 'most trusted envoy' to visit Peking for talks. Nixon was willing to hold parleys in utmost secrecy, as he wanted the White House to establish direct contact with the CCP leadership so that he could personally control the line of communication without interference from outside, especially the State Department. Yahya readily agreed to play the role. In April 1970, the Chinese agreed to receive Nixon's most 'trusted envoy'.

To hoodwink the world and elude prying eyes, in early July, Henry Kissinger, Nixon's National Security Adviser, embarked on a so-called 'fact-finding tour' of five Asian nations. He landed in Delhi on 7 July and what he said and did in Delhi engaged the attention of the leaders of the government in exile camping in Calcutta. He held extensive talks with the close advisers of Mrs Gandhi, especially P.N. Haksar and D.P. Dhar, on the developing scenario in Bangladesh. It was during his interaction with P.N. Haksar that Kissinger said that in case of an Indo-Pak armed conflict, with China intervening on behalf of Pakistan, America would be 'severely constrained' from providing any kind of assistance to India.

What he left unsaid was that America would side with Pakistan and China in case of such an eventuality, thereby conveying a veiled threat to India. This came as a rude shock to the Indian advisers of Mrs Gandhi, who could not believe their ears and requested him to restate what he had said. That a democratic America would side with the world's most bloodthirsty military dictator of the worst kind and a monolithic Chinese Communist regime rather than with the world's largest democracy was incredible to them. Alarm bells started ringing both in Delhi and Moscow. India's foreign policy planners could not believe that America's policy towards China had already undergone a sea change and that far greater surprises were waiting to unfold in the next few days, which they could not even conceive of. What Kissinger had told them was, however, just a curtain raiser to far greater dramatic and hair-raising developments that would soon get unravelled. General Yahya would be a key player in these developments. It was a role for which Nixon would ever remain beholden to Yahya.

Neither the Indians nor the Soviets had the foggiest idea that Kissinger's forthcoming Islamabad visit between 9-11 July was a ruse to help him reach Peking secretly to hold direct talks with the CCP leadership. He feigned sickness at a state banquet in Islamabad and was supposedly transferred to a neighbouring hill station in a decoy government limousine for 'rest and to be left alone there for the next three days'. This aroused no suspicion in Delhi and other world capitals. None had the faintest idea that this ploy, code-named 'Operation Marco Polo', was a diversionary tactic to help Kissinger board a special PIA flight, without any other passenger, from a Pakistani military airfield to Peking. The entire operation was kept under a tight veil of secrecy and known only to Yahya and his personal driver, who drove Kissinger to the airport.

During his three-day stay in Peking, Kissinger had hectic rounds of discussion with the Chinese leadership but mostly with Premier Zhou Enlai. According to declassified Congressional documents, the main focus of their discussion centred around Taiwan, the 'expansionist' moves made by the Soviets the world over, and also on improving Sino-US ties. Zhou also made a series of disparaging remarks against India, its former prime minister Jawaharlal Nehru and his famous book, *The Discovery of India*. The declassified documents including the minutes of the Kissinger-Zhou discussion make fascinating reading because it lays bare the deep animus of the top Chinese Communist leadership towards India. It also exposes the lies that Zhou had sought to feed Kissinger against India. He repeatedly tried to project China as a 'victim' of the 1962 'Indian aggression' and said that his country was prepared for such attacks in future to be launched by India on a 'bigger scale'. He also said that the 'Indian propaganda' on East Pakistan suggested that it would launch a strike against Pakistan soon and welcomed Kissinger's initiative in 'warning India' not to tread such a path during his Delhi visit.

Peking also doubted the Kremlin's honesty and sincerity about working out a peaceful settlement on East Pakistan and said that whatever it was doing in this direction now was a sham and 'superficial'. Kissinger was asked: 'Didn't the Soviets in 1965 issue the "so-called" Tashkent declaration?' Zhou was unhappy that the Soviets were supplying military equipment to India on a big scale, which would turn it into an 'expansionist' nation. Interestingly Kissinger countered Zhou with the pointed question about China too supplying arms to Pakistan. According to those documents, Zhou justified the supply saying, 'We are giving arms to Pakistan because India is committing aggression against it just as it did against us in 1962.' He then indirectly complimented Kissinger for branding India as an 'aggressor' during the 1962 Sino-Indian conflict in course of their discussion. Kissinger cut Zhou short and corrected him saying: 'No, not me. You said that.'

Undeterred by this mild snub, Zhou became more aggressive. He said that South Asia was in turmoil and 'the situation there is not normalizing, largely because of India'. He held India wholly responsible for the growing tension in the region, especially in East Pakistan. Then he turned his ire against 'the so-called Bangladesh headquarters set up in India'. 'Isn't that a subversion of Pakistan government's authority? We can't but pay attention to this and China's attention will be much greater than that of the U.S. because the issue is being played out just before our eyes. We have to be prepared for 1962 like aggression,' Zhou said, according to those documents.

It was not until 15 July that the US media announced that Zhou Enlai had extended an official invitation to President Nixon to visit China. That was when the world came to know that Kissinger had secretly visited Peking during his Islamabad trip, held several rounds of wide-ranging discussion, including turmoil in South Asia, with the top leadership of the Chinese Communist Party. Kissinger's secret trip to Peking came as a shocker both to the Indian and Soviet leaderships. Indian leaders, like their Soviet counterparts, viewed this as an 'ominous development'. Both sides were suspicious that Kissinger and the Chinese had hatched a 'sinister' plan against India to subvert Bangladesh's liberation struggle and to have the whole of South Asia under their hegemonic control. The attitude of indifference and disdain with which an influential section of the Indian leadership had treated Marshal Grechko's offer of signing a treaty of friendship and co-operation with India underwent a sea change overnight. It was replaced with an urgent need to conclude an agreement at the earliest on the suggested Soviet line.

Many were heard complaining about Sardar Swaran Singh's disappointing role in spurning the 'generous' Soviet offer of underwriting India's 'total' security, should either China or Pakistan, or both jointly, attack it. It was widely felt India could not have asked for anything better than what the Soviets had offered, to provide 'unqualified help'. The offer extended to 'accepting total responsibility of defending India, which would devolve on them because of the commitment to be made in the friendship treaty'. At a time when, diplomatically, India was in a tight corner on the Bangladesh issue, not accepting the Soviet offer, which it had not asked for, and with no alternative in sight, would be unwise.

Marshal Grechko had assured Dhar that the Soviet military would 'at once go to India's assistance if any of the two countries tried to indulge in any kind of overt or covert armed adventurism against India'. Such a treaty, according to the Soviet defence minister, 'would not only act as a deterrent against forces inimical to India but would also go a long way in demonstrating to them the solidarity in relations that existed between the two countries. Nothing could be better for Indo-Soviet relations than a friendship treaty, based on mutual help and trust,' he had told Dhar.

The Kissinger episode triggered a tectonic shift in India's foreign policy and the way it was conducting its international diplomacy. The non-aligned foreign policy of maintaining equidistance from two contending power blocs, scrupulously pursued since the Nehru era, was dumped. In the next few weeks, there were fast-paced developments both in Moscow and Delhi, which took both China and the West by surprise. Without any loss of time, Mrs Gandhi rushed D.P. Dhar to Moscow on 2 August, to pursue the Friendship Treaty offer and find out whether it was still on. Dhar also had a second agenda to discuss: that Delhi was willing to accord recognition to Bangladesh on 9 August. Hearing this, the Soviet foreign minister, Andre Gromyko, air dashed to Delhi on 7 August, to hold 'urgent consultations' with Indian leaders. He assured them that the Soviet treaty offer still held good. He, however, persuaded Indian leaders to withhold recognition of Bangladesh for the present, cautioning that it would certainly escalate tension between India and Pakistan and complicate matters internationally.

The Indo-Soviet Treaty

The Indo-Soviet Treaty of Peace and Friendship and Co-operation was signed in Delhi on 9 August by Andre Gromyko and Sardar Swaran Singh. The treaty's signing was hastened by Yahya's nationwide radio and televised broadcast announcing that Mujib would be tried and 'justly punished' by a secret military court for committing 'treason' against the state of Pakistan. Such a trial of a popular mass leader, if held, would be a farce and considered to be a travesty of justice. Mrs Gandhi was at the forefront of world leaders who demanded Mujib's immediate release as only that could facilitate the holding of a negotiated settlement for restoring peace and tranquility in East Pakistan. UN Secretary General U. Thant's public expression of 'serious concern' for the 'threat to Mujib's life and well-being' generated fresh anxiety and heightened it to no end. But the signing of the Indo-Soviet treaty helped in sobering down Yahya's aggressive posturing on Mujib.

The friendship treaty was to remain in force for 20 years. The most important clause of the loosely worded treaty said that in case of a military attack 'its signatories would come to each other's assistance immediately'. A few days after the treaty was signed, Gromyko happened to meet the Pak foreign secretary, Sultan Mohammed Khan, whom he warned saying: 'Do not do anything which would oblige us to fulfil our commitment towards the country with which we have a friendship treaty.' Gurginov had informed many of us that the Chinese diplomats, especially the defense attaches posted in South Asian capitals, were also informed by their Soviet counterparts about the Soviet treaty obligations in clear and unambiguous terms. This was because, according to Gurginov, the Nixon administration had asked China to mass its troops along the Indian border in Arunachal and Ladakh to keep India in check. The Chinese had viewed the agreement as something directed against them. The Soviets, in their diplomatic parleys, made no secret of this being really their objective.

The Soviets stalling India's move to recognize Bangladesh deepened the despondency in the provisional government circles. It emboldened the Mushtaq group to openly pass snide remarks against Mrs Gandhi and India. The point that they were hammering at was that neither India nor the Soviets was interested in translating Bangabandhu's dream into reality. A sizable section of the government led by Tajuddin, however, saw a silver lining in the signing of the treaty, as India, with Soviet support behind it, would be able to act more decisively and confidently on the Bangladesh issue. When Mrs Gandhi followed up the signing of the treaty by visiting Moscow in September and persuaded the Kremlin leaders to agree that a military rather than a peacefully negotiated solution held the key to resolving the Bangladesh issue, broad smiles appeared on the worried faces of Tajuddin Ahmed and Syed Nazrul Islam at long last.

During her two and a half days stay in Moscow, Mrs Gandhi had done some plain speaking with the Soviet leaders, when she discovered that Soviet Premier Kosygin had an ambivalent attitude towards Pakistan and was thinking in favour of resuming limited arms supplies to Islamabad as a possible stratagem to rein in Yahya. Mr Subimal Dutt, India's first high commissioner in Bangladesh (a former Indian foreign secretary and an ex-Indian envoy to Moscow), shared this interesting episode of Mrs Gandhi's visit to Moscow with me much later. Possible resumption of Soviet arms shipment to Pakistan had irked Mrs Gandhi so much that she asked Kosygin point blank whether he supported the Indian stand to send back the refugees with honour, dignity and respect to an independent sovereign Bangladesh at the earliest or wanted Yahya to continue with his killing spree by renewing arms supplies to Yahya.

She feared that if the Soviets supplied arms to Pakistan, it would not only prolong India's agony with the refugees but that would also help in sustaining the Yahya regime and encourage it to continue with its programme of indulging in more mass killings. The Soviet leadership was bluntly asked to make a clean choice between losing a prospective alliance partner like India in South Asia or courting a nation like Pakistan, which was already a long-standing ally of the US and had the best of relations with its all-weather friend, China. This no-nonsense message from Mrs Gandhi forced the Soviet leadership to fully come around to the Indian stand and shed its ambivalence towards Pakistan and lend 'total support' to India's Bangladesh policy.

To demonstrate to the Indian leadership and their people that Soviet Union was one with the Indian stance on the Bangladesh issue and to express its solidarity with India, Soviet President Nikolai V. Podgorny made an unscheduled longish stopover in Delhi on his way to Hanoi, within two days of Mrs Gandhi's return home from Moscow. His visit was not only an expression and show of support to India but also meant to reassure Delhi that Moscow had, indeed, revised its policy on East Pakistan and would remain steadfast in its commitment made in the Friendship Treaty.

Meanwhile, the months of July, August and September had seen a sudden spurt in the hit-and-run raids on Pakistani military posts and convoys. With India-based camps having trained almost 9,000 Mukti Bahini men for waging guerilla war inside Bangladesh, it was high time to send them in larger numbers on missions for which they had been trained. Reports of successive daring raids by

Mukti Bahini's intrepid naval commandos on Pakistani vessels and gunboats, deployed to patrol the sea and the main riverine ports, as also the daring exploits of the Mukti Bahini on land, were getting wide coverage in the Indian media.

It was on Pakistan Day, 14 August, that my photographer colleague from *The Statesman*, Shyamadas Basu, and I had our close brush with death. We had boarded a big boat loaded with freedom fighters at Jalangi in Murshidabad on the Padma river. They were going on a daring operation to attack the Pakistan Police Academy at Sarda, in Rajshahi, on the riverbank. The Pak military was holding an investiture ceremony there, to be followed by a *burra khana* (feast) for the troops. The police academy had earned considerable notoriety for having been turned into an interrogation-cum-torture centre of captured freedom fighters. So it was under the radar of the Mukti Bahini for a targeted attack. Some heavily armed commandos of the BSF had also boarded the boat as a backup. The mission was highly risky because the academy was heavily guarded by the military. The plan was to drop the *muktijoddha*s, all experts in long-distance swimming, some distance from the shore of the academy and wait for their return to the boat in the dark moonless night after they had completed their grenade lobbying operation.

The widest stretch of the river was already in spate because of the heavy monsoon rains. It was selected for river crossing to avoid easy detection. After crossing mid-stream, the freedom fighters received coats of grease and black paint on their faces and bodies. As they silently slipped into the swirling waters one by one and began swimming towards the shore lit by the academy's floodlights, we waited with bated breath and began praying for the success of the mission and their safe return. Their rendezvous point with their local guide was a village adjoining the academy. The boat dropped its anchor and stood still, some distance away from mid-stream. It was pitch dark and silence prevailed all around. Except the gurgling noise from the river's swirling waters, perfect peace and calm reigned. We thought that the pervading darkness had provided us with perfect cover. We were mistaken.

Suddenly and unexpectedly a hail of bullets flew over our heads. We lay flat on our stomachs on the wooden floor of the giant rowboat. Soon there appeared from nowhere a motorized gunboat with powerful headlights and light machine guns, focusing its headlight and fire on our boat. Showers of bullets flew menacingly overhead, forcing us to remain motionless for how long, I do not remember. We lay thus, scared stiff, in that position. The LMG fire had sprung leaks in our wooden boat but the return fusillade, from a host of grenade launchers that the BSF commandos were carrying, silenced the Pakistani fire and sent the gunboat up in a ball of fire. It was just like in the movies. The Mukti Bahini commander, seeing more gunboats with powerful searchlights heading towards us, aborted the mission and asked the boatmen to row our boat furiously towards Jalangi.

While returning to Jalangi, we discovered that one of the freedom fighters on board had been hit by Pak gunfire and sustained serious injuries in his hand. Hearing the Pakistani firing and seeing a boat burning mid-stream, the BSF mechanized gunboats with searchlights came to our rescue. The freedom fighters who had swum ashore to Sarda for their daring operation swam back to Jalangi early next morning as the Pak military was swarming all over the academy. The freedom fighters were under strict instructions not to confront the military because of their superior firepower.

Decisive Phase

India's Information and Broadcasting Ministry then launched a morale-boosting initiative. It instructed the Calcutta and Agartala stations of All India Radio to broadcast the valiant deeds of Mukti Bahini in their regular programmes. It also started playing coded songs in Bengali, which were actually signals to freedom fighters inside Bangladesh to launch attacks on the Pakistani targets. Its news commentary on the liberation war and the Mukti Bahini onslaughts on the Pakistan military made the Bengalis of Bangladesh remain glued to the radio for certain hours of the day. Some programmes aired by Swadhin Bangla Betar Kendro also became so popular that they became the staple of every Bengali's daily life. This brought cheer and lifted the spirits of not only the disheartened Bangladeshis in India but also those living inside Bangladesh. Clear signs were emerging that the liberation war was gradually entering its final and decisive phase.

The entire stretch of the Passur and Karnaphuli rivers, connecting the Chalna and Chittagong ports with the sea, had been heavily mined by the Bahini's naval commandos at breakneck speed. That prevented any foreign enemy naval vessel from entering Bangladesh waters. This task was performed under the watchful eye of the Indian Navy's ace frogman, Chiman Singh Yadav. Sector commanders like Majors Khaled Mosharraf, A.T.M. Hyder, Rafiqul Islam, Abu Osman Choudhury, who led their men from the front, had been so successful in their roles that the Pakistanis avoided going in for a direct confrontation against them in sectors under their charge. Those commanders had caused unimaginable damage to the entire infrastructure of East Pakistan. Economically it was in a shambles. All forms of communication, including road, rail and telecom, had been badly disrupted.

According to stragglers coming from Dacca their city looked like a ghost town after dusk with no one venturing outdoors. The only vehicles seen on the road belonged to the military with heavily armed soldiers in them. At night the city reverberated with sounds of gunfire and grenade explosions. This was because Major Khaled Mosharraf and Hyder used to plan and execute their derring-do raids on Dacca so suddenly and at such lightning speed that every time the Pakistanis were caught unawares. They were always kept guessing about when and from where the next attack would come. This element of shock and surprise became the hallmark of their well-planned guerilla raids. The freedom fighters had been able to infiltrate even into the city's upmarket residential areas like Dhan Mandi and Gulshan, wherein they had found safe houses for themselves from where they operated.

Calcutta had already become a hotbed for espionage and counter espionage, and much later I had the good fortune to learn of some of them courtesy of Mrs Jayanti Ghosh, daughter of former chief of BSF's eastern frontier, Golak Majumdar, and his very close friend Nihar Chakravarty who had provided food for the famished Bangladesh prime minister on the night of his arrival to the city. It was the same Chakravarty who had tipped off Golak Majumdar about having noticed something 'sinister and unusual' on his early morning walk down Theatre Road. He had seen sophisticated cameras and electronic devices hanging out of the glass window of one of the rooms of the topmost floor of a five-star hotel overlooking

Tajuddin Ahmed's office-cum-residence bungalow in Theatre Road. All the gadgets were directed at Tajuddin's bungalow. He had also noticed strange foreigners, never seen before in the area, so early in the morning, walking to and fro, in front of the gates of 8, Theatre Road, in a suspicious manner. Nihar Chakravarty's instinct told him that they were foreign security men waiting to nab someone who would come out of the bungalow.

Nihar had seen this on successive mornings. He rang up Golak to inform him that something 'highly suspicious' was happening outside Tajuddin Ahmed's bungalow early in the morning. On some days, Nihar had seen Tajuddin coming out of the bungalow and heading straight for the neighbouring Maidan for his early morning walk. Usually, he would do his morning exercise and walk within the vast compound of the bungalow. Golak promptly dispatched a team of his sleuths to the five-star hotel only to find that those living in the room had run away in panic, leaving their snooping devices and even personal belongings behind. Those were seized and an examination of those devices revealed that the Americans had been keeping a close watch on Tajuddin for over a month, especially his movements throughout the day. Their main focus was on what he did early in the morning; his exercise drill and walk.

Golak wondered what the purpose of gathering such information on Tajuddin could be. Why should strange-looking foreigners conduct their morning walk in front of this bungalow at 5 am? Checking the identity of the foreigners, he soon found out that the 'strange' foreigners were American Marines, recently flown into the city for an 'unspecified purpose'. It was 'certainly not for guarding American life and property or interests in the city'. Golak started digging with his sources in the American administration and intelligence and only after the liberation of Bangladesh did he find out that, in desperation, the Nixon administration had hatched a plot to kidnap Tajuddin.

The idea was to kidnap the Bangladesh prime minister during his morning walk and bundle him into a waiting helicopter in Calcutta's Maidan area and fly him out of India to an aircraft carrier, stationed in the Bay of Bengal. The Nixon administration felt that, if its plan succeeded, the provisional Bangladesh government would be like a headless chicken and elements like Khondokar Mushtaq would be activated to prevent the emergence of Bangladesh and save Pakistan from the inevitability of a break-up.

Over the months of July, August and September, India witnessed groundswell of support from its people for Indira Gandhi's Bangladesh policy. Bengalis of West Bengal were so emotionally overwhelmed by her steadfast and firm stand to defend the democratic rights of Bengalis of East Bengal that she became the theme of many of the prominent *pujo pandals* of Calcutta. Idols of Durga were modelled on Mrs Gandhi's face and that of Mahishashur the demon was modelled on Yahya, in his military outfit. The Indian prime minister was shown decapitating the Pak president with her trident. To attract crowds, some *pandals* hung banners outside stating, '*Maa Indirar Yahya badh dekhte bhetoray aashun*' (Come in to see Mother Indira slaying Yahya). There was the unprecedented sprouting of 'Bangladesh solidarity committees' and 'Friends of Bangladesh' groups all over the city, even amongst professional performing groups. They raised funds by staging musical concerts and art shows for Bangladeshi refugees. The Indian postal department made it mandatory to affix a five-paise stamp on every postal item sent within or outside the country. The money, thus raised, went into the government coffers for refugee relief work.

Ravi Shankar and Bangladesh

In early July, the sitar maestro Pandit Ravi Shankar visited Calcutta when he participated in a concert to raise funds for Bangladesh. It was during his stay in the city that he learnt that the Pak military had burnt down the ancestral home of his father, Shyamsundar Chowdhury, in Mymensingh in East Pakistan. More than saddened, he was incensed with the information and wanted to lodge a global protest, by holding an international musical concert in which the world's iconic musical stars would participate, and focus on the ongoing genocide in East Pakistan, the land of his forefathers. He shared his plan with some of his close confidants in Calcutta and all of them supported his proposed venture.

He then broached the idea to George Harrison, the lead guitarist of The Beatles. Harrison immediately grabbed his 'guru's' idea and approached legendary singers like Eric Clapton, Bob Dylan and Joan Baez to be the active participants of the concert. He booked New York's Madison Square Garden with a seating capacity of 21,000 for his 1 August, Bangladesh concert. Tickets for the show were an instant sellout. The concert had generated so much interest among the music lovers worldwide that a couple of thousands flew into New York for the event.

The Madison Square Garden overflowed with international music lovers from various parts of the world and chants of 'I love Bangladesh' rented the air. The concert started with an emotive introduction from

Pandit Ravi Shankar who said, 'I belong to East Bengal and have close affinity with its people. Today's concert is an attempt to secure the world's attention through music to the grisly barbarities being committed on its people by a ruthless junta. I think this concert will change the perspective from which the world has so far been seeing the horrible happenings there.' The lyrics of George Harrison's theme song – 'Bangladesh' – were so moving and its tune so gripping that they were on everybody's lips in New York and elsewhere in America in the following days and weeks. And subsequently all over the world.

What international diplomacy could not achieve for Bangladesh for the last four months, one night's concert did. It familiarized the world with Bangladesh's agony in an international outreach to get the world to stand by the Bengalis. On the same day, London's Trafalgar Square was witness to a protest rally by 25,000 people demanding 'immediate stoppage of mass killings and recognition of Bangladesh'. Organized by 'Action Bangladesh', it was headed by an English schoolteacher and an Oxford graduate, both of whom went to the Pakistan High Commission in London with a Bangladesh flag and started chanting the Bengali war cry '*Joy Bangla*' and read out a declaration proclaiming Bangladesh's independence.

Both the events received enormous international publicity and the Bangladesh problem became a hot topic of discussion across the world. There was realization that this was no 'strange, obscure or goddamned back of the beyond place' where Pakistan's barbarities would go unnoticed. Its problem deserved immediate world attention and resolution. These developments swung the mood of the Calcutta-based Bangladesh leadership. What perked up spirits further was the deployment of seven divisions of the Indian military with armour, artillery and APCs along the East Pakistan border. In order to facilitate operations by IAF fighter jets, Calcutta airport's passenger flights remained closed for certain hours of the day.

Editors of newspaper offices in Calcutta started receiving letters from the defence ministry seeking names of reporters whom they would nominate as war correspondents to report for their dailies straight from the battlefield if a war broke out in East Pakistan. My editor nominated me as one of the four war correspondents.

Diplomatic circles in Delhi and Calcutta and several world capitals were also agog with a subtle diplomatic move made by General Yahya to internationalize the Bangladesh issue. He suggested that the United Nations be asked to place several thousand UN observers and UNHCR functionaries all along the East Pakistan-India border to monitor and report on the goings on along the entire 4,000-km stretch of the international border. Nixon approved the idea and UN Secretary General U. Thant gave a go-ahead to Yahya's proposal. Mrs Gandhi strongly rejected the move questioning how it would facilitate a lasting political settlement in East Pakistan, which could be ensured only by freeing Mujib and working out a political settlement with him.

Yahya was emboldened to internationalize the issue because the then Indian high commissioner in Islamabad J.K. Atal told the Pakistani president that Mujib's release was not a necessary pre-condition for holding talks as he was no longer important in finding a solution to the Bangladesh issue. According to Ashoke Roy, the head of the Calcutta branch secretariat of MEA, Atal and the then Indian foreign secretary, 'Tikky' N. Kaul, did not 'see eye to eye on many foreign policy issues'. The former had on some occasions sought to subtly undercut South Block's Bangladesh policy in the past. I could not ascertain whether Atal was a lone ranger pursuing this bizarre line, which was diametrically opposed to the official policy, or he had the backing of an influential lobby in South Block. Mr Roy asked me not to report this 'deplorable episode' as it would immensely harm India's national interest.

Meanwhile, brushing aside Soviet objections, Indira Gandhi visited Washington for holding direct talks with Nixon in mid-November with three objectives in view. She wanted Nixon to exert pressure on Yahya to release Mujib and negotiate a peaceful political solution. She also wanted Nixon to mount pressure on the Pakistani president to take back all the 15 million refugees who had sought shelter in India since 25 March. She held extensive discussions with the US president but, as the declassified US archives show, he was unwilling to accede to any of her three demands. Instead he pressed her hard to withdraw Indian troops from both the borders of East and West Pakistan and agree to the stationing of thousands of UN observers along the India-East Pakistan frontier. Declassified archival papers say that Nixon had dismissed the refugee issue as not meriting immediate attention, though he agreed to increase the quantum of American relief for the Bangladesh refugees. During Mrs Gandhi's stay in Washington, Nixon's officials leaked to the press that he was seriously mulling over a series of proposals including suspension of all kinds of aid to India. This incensed Mrs Gandhi so much that she told the US media that attempts to pressurize India to abandon the Mukti Bahini would not succeed and that India would ensure that efforts by Mukti Bahini to liberate Bangladesh did not fail. Her statement was followed by the US cutting off all kinds of aid to India. She told the American people and media that she had come to their country 'looking for a deeper understanding of the worsening situation in our part of the world'. But her Washington visit had dashed all those hopes. She was returning to Delhi empty handed. On 7 November 1971, *The New York Times* editorially commented on Indira Gandhi's Washington visit questioning Nixon's wisdom of 'losing the goodwill of 550 million Indians for the sake of mere 150 million Pakistanis'.

On her return to Delhi, she told the US envoy, Kenneth Keating, that his president had failed to scare India from supporting Bangladesh and that on the refugee issue the Indian patience was wearing thin. 'I can't hold it back any longer. It is giving away.' Swaran Singh told Keating: 'Even at this late hour if Yahya released Mujib in a dramatic gesture, a settlement could be reached.' But Yahya had already geared himself for a war as he had told his friends and admirers that he would not be available for the next three or four days since he would be at the battlefront leading the Pakistani charge against India. This comment was widely reported in the world media.

Two days later, on 21 November, a fierce tank battle was fought at Garibpur near Bongaon-Boyra axis along the India-East Pakistan border. The Indian armoured battalion of PT 74 Russian amphibious tanks had fought a brigade-strong America-made Patton and Chaffee tanks, outmanoeuvering and outgunning them in a two-and-a-half-hour-long battle. Three Pakistani Sabre jets, which had come to the aid of the tank brigade, were shot down. Garibpur became a graveyard of American tanks not seen ever before in the post-World War II era. As *The Statesman*'s war correspondent, I reached the battlefront in the evening to find burnt hulk of the Pakistani armour still spewing dense black smoke. Bloodied bodies of the Pakistani tank crew were being taken out from the tanks. The next morning, the entire international press corps based in Calcutta was taken to Garibpur to highlight that the Pakistani tanks had in fact entered Indian territory to launch an offensive and the Pak fighters too had violated the Indian air space and had been shot down well inside Indian territory.

Kissinger and Will Rogers, Secretary of State, demanded that India immediately disengage its forces. Mrs Gandhi's riposte was 'even if India disengaged, it would leave the basic situation on ground in East Pakistan unchanged. We cannot listen to advice that weakens us. We have to look after our national interest' (Declassified US Archive records). Yahya indicated in press interviews that in case of war breaking out 'Pakistan's posture' would be 'offensive and not defensive'. Indian strategic experts expected him to launch an attack on Kashmir to take pressure off East Pakistan and West Pakistan borders. Nixon warned Mrs Gandhi that his government was not being tough enough on Indian transgressions and, if India precipitated an attack, it would be viewed adversely both by his government and the American people. Meanwhile, Yahya again threatened publicly that if 'that woman' (meaning Mrs Gandhi) forced the refugees to go back to East Pakistan, he would unleash a 'total war' on India.

The New York Times correspondent Sydney Schanberg in his Calcutta dateline story of 25 November reported that he had seen Indian troops crossing the Indo-East Pakistan border with armour. Warren Unna's reports from Washington appearing in *The Statesman* said that the White House aides thought Yahya with only two weeks of ammunition supplies left would not be able to defend East Pakistan for more than two weeks and that too without India deploying its air force. They thought Moscow could militarily reinforce India faster than China to Pakistan, which drastically tilted the military balance in India's favour. *The Stateman*'s Beirut-based West Asian correspondent, G.H. Jansen, a former officer in the Indian Army, quoted Israeli sources buttressing those facts, in one of his dispatches. Even when Mrs Gandhi found America and China were teaming up at the UN Security Council to force India to disengage its forces and allow the posting of thousands of UN observers on the India-East Pakistan border, she refused to attack Pakistan first.

She was greatly relieved then, when Pakistan became the official aggressor by carrying out pre-emptive air strikes on nine Indian air bases on the afternoon of 3 December in northern and western India just when Mrs Gandhi was addressing a massive public rally at Calcutta's Brigade Parade Ground. She cut short her speech by publicly announcing that Pakistan had attacked India. I was at the rally listening to her mesmerizing speech. The moment she came down from the dais and got into her car, slogans eulogizing her courage and leadership were raised all over the ground both in Bengali and Hindi. She hurried back to Delhi to hold an important cabinet meeting at midnight. In a memorable address to the nation on 4 December 1971 over All India Radio whose transcript is as follows she said:

> A war has been forced on us. We repeatedly drew the world's attention to the annihilation of an entire people whose only crime was that it had voted democratically. But the world ignored the basic causes and concerned itself with certain repercussions. Most governments and people the world over showed sympathy and understanding to the dangers that India and Bangladesh were faced with. But they seemed morally and politically paralyzed to take action. The situation was bound to deteriorate and the courageous band of freedom fighters have been staking their all in defense of the values for which we have also struggled and which are basic to our way of life. Today, war on Bangladesh has become war on India and this imposes upon me, my government and the people, an awesome responsibility. We are left with no other option but to put our country on a war footing. I have no doubt the united will of our people will decisively repel this wanton and unprovoked Pakistani aggression with fortitude.

Indira Gandhi's address had a galvanizing effect on the Indian masses and all sections of Bangladeshis living in and outside India. Many Bangladeshi couples living in India started naming their newborn daughters Indira. The trend was set by a leading and much respected Dacca columnist, Abdul Ghaffar Chowdhury, then staying in Calcutta with his family. For the first time, I heard a leading Bangladeshi barrister, Sirajul Haque, an Awami League MNA from Comilla's Kasba constituency, and his wife likening Mrs Gandhi to '*Maa Durga*'. Mrs Haque said Mrs Gandhi was '*Sakhkhat Maa Durga*' (Goddess Durga reincarnate) and that she started her day by seeking her *dua* (blessings). Such was the image of Mrs Gandhi even among discerning Bangladeshis.

The Indian prime minister's address was enough indication that India would hit back hard at points that hurt Pakistan the most. Taking advantage of the full moon, on 4 December, the IAF bombers carried out massive bombing raids on Dacca's Kurmitola air base making its runway and a squadron of Sabre jets parked there unserviceable. Chittagong and Lalmonirhat air bases were also bombed, thereby grounding the entire PAF jet squadrons. *INS Vikrant*'s fleet of air arm carried out raids on the Cox's Bazaar airfield. Thus India gained complete air dominance over East Pakistan. The daring rocket attack by Indian Navy's missile boats on the Karachi harbour oil depots rendered them totally inoperative as well. The sinking of one third of the Pakistani naval fleet raised concerns both in Washington and Beijing that Pakistan would not be able to defend itself neither in the east, nor in the west.

Both the US and China, with the help of some other members, launched an intense diplomatic offensive to corner India at the UN. Both convened a meeting of the UN Security Council (UNSC) to demand an immediate ceasefire and disengagement of forces along the India-Pakistan border. The permanent Chinese representative, Huang Hua, launched a blistering attack on India for 'playing a most insidious role in South Asia by stripping off its cloak of non-alliance and joining hands with Soviet Socialist imperialism' (*Bangladesh Document* [1971-72]). He was hopping mad with India's UN permanent representative Samar Sen's rejection of the ceasefire proposal. Samar Sen's stand, that unless the UNSC formally heard the Bangladesh representative's side of the story of happenings in his country, the ceasefire proposal would be irrelevant, made Huang Hua angrier.

The fact was that Pakistan was against any negotiation with the secessionist elements. Both the US and the Chinese representatives kept pressing for immediate ceasefire, which was thrice vetoed by the Soviet Union. This provoked Bhutto to say in frustration, 'Let's build a monument for veto in the UN to demonstrate the impotence and incapacity of this international body. But we shall continue to wage a thousand years war against India, if needed' (ibid.).

On 6 December, after the fall of the important cantonment town of Jessore, India recognized Bangladesh. Announcing her government's decision in parliament, Mrs Gandhi said Dacca was now the capital of a free, sovereign, independent Bangladesh. There was merriment on the streets of Calcutta with mikes blaring '*Aamar Sonar Bangla*' and '*Shono ekti Mujiburer theke lakhya Mujiburer kantha*' cassettes and people distributing sweets and many residents hoisting Bangladeshi flags on their housetops.

Moscow had been persistently urging Delhi to wrap up its military campaign by securing Dacca's fall at the earliest. Otherwise it would be difficult to withstand the diplomatic pressure to be unleashed jointly by the US, China and Britain to stall the rapid advance of the Indian military and avert the fall of Dacca by calling for an immediate ceasefire. Accordingly, in a masterstroke, the Indian Army outflanked the heavily defended Pakistani positions by surrounding them on all sides and forcing them to surrender. It did not want to get bogged down in prolonged battles as it wanted to reach Dacca fast. Indian paratroopers, airdropped around Tangail, took rickshaws and walked on foot as no other transport was available to take them to Dacca. Indian troops crossed the Madhumati and Meghna rivers in hundreds of country boats and launches as there were few helicopters to help them cross the two mighty rivers. The IAF's rocket attack on the Governor's House in Dacca on 14 December, forced Governor Abdul Malek to seek refuge in a Red Cross camp. Overnight, the scene changed dramatically.

The fast-paced Indian advance, coupled with Mukti Bahini's daring assaults on Pakistani positions around Dacca, robbed the Pakistanis of their will to fight. Their spirits were briefly buoyed up by reports of Nixon dispatching the US Navy's 7th fleet to the Bay of Bengal on 10 December and of Kissinger asking Beijing to amass troops along the Ladakh border. The British aircraft carrier *HMS Eagle* too had been dispatched to Indian waters with orders to attack Indian vessels if the situation warranted. With the entire Soviet Pacific fleet, including nuclear submarines, tailing the US and British warships, both the western navies beat a hasty retreat. It was the presence of the Soviet fleet that tilted the military balance in India's favour. Otherwise, the history of Bangladesh might have been quite different.

Indian jawans had started trickling into Dacca from the morning of 15 December. On the 16th morning there were only about 3,000 Indian troops in the city whereas the strength of the Pakistanis was beyond 25,000. Repeated ultimatum served to the Pakistanis by General Manekshaw to surrender had demoralized them so much that putting up any further resistance to Indian advance was beyond their realm of possibility. That they would capitulate and surrender in a matter of hours had almost become a certainty.

Battle for Khulna

I could not be in Dacca to witness the Pakistani surrender on 16 December, as I had been assigned to move as an embedded journalist with the 9th mountain division led by Major General Dalbir Singh, who was pursuing a Pakistani brigade in his bid to capture Khulna. The Pak brigade commander, Brigadier Hyat Khan, had dug himself in Daulatpur, in Khulna's outskirts. For four successive days, Hyat had stalled the Indian advance at Phultala, inflicting heavy casualties. For five nights, I was stuck in Phultala as Brig. Hyat just would not give up fighting. General Dalbir sent several messages to him saying it was pointless to fight even after General Niazi had surrendered in Dacca and a ceasefire had come into force.

Then in a sudden, dramatic gesture, flying a white flag on his Toyota Land Cruiser, Hyat drove up to General Dalbir's camp headquarters to inform him that he and his troops would surrender to him. There were batchmates of Hyat in the 9th mountain division, who had done military courses together in various military colleges and training establishments in pre-Partition India. They warmly hugged and swooped each other up as they would do in their younger days. To me it seemed that they were long-lost cousins who were reuniting in strange and difficult circumstances after a long time. While counting their losses and gains in the Khulna battle, they displayed an unusual bonhomie by using choicest and popular Punjabi expletives to highlight how hard they had been at each other during the battle.

Justifying the fierce fight that he and his men had put up, Hyat told General Dalbir that he had been given the 'wrong impression' by Dacca's Eastern Command that the American 7th fleet would come to his brigade's rescue and evacuate its men to waiting US naval ships. When he found out that the American fleet had begun steaming away from the bay, it was pointless to continue the fight. Moreover, it was more honourable to surrender to 'brother Indian Army' than die an ignominious death by getting slaughtered by the Mukti Bahini guerillas. He had seen how the Mukti Bahini had slaughtered countless Bihari *razakar*s, whose bodies were strewn all over the Khulna-Jessore Road. All had their throats slit and stomachs disembowelled. His brother officers and men had seen the ghastly sight and did not want to die 'such an inglorious, horrible and unsoldierly death'.

Without wasting time, he wanted to surrender to the Indian Army. General Dalbir heard Hyat's reasons for surrendering quietly and intently and then invited other Pakistani officers of the brigade to come over and help themselves to a sumptuous lunch of mutton biriyani and chicken *chaap* (chicken in a thick gravy) that had been specially cooked for the occasion. Hundreds of cans and bottles of imported and local beer were taken out of freezer chests, opened up and offered to the Pakistanis so that they could drink to their heart's content in the Indian officers' mess tent. All were treated with respect and dignity befitting their rank and seniority.

The Pakistani officers felt so much at ease in the company of 'brother' Indian officers that I heard them repeatedly requesting, '*Yaar aur ek beer ka can ho jaye. Bahut pyas hai*' (Pass another beer can, my friend. I am very thirsty). Young Indian lieutenants and captains in their black tank crew outfits went scampering to the beer counter to get chilled beer cans for them. I was so amazed by this camaraderie that I was provoked to ask Brig. Hyat, 'What was the last five days' fight for? Why did you fight so hard and to what purpose?' His reply was: 'Don't ask me. Ask Gen. Niazi and our president.' At 4 pm, Brig. Hyat and his brigade laid down their arms in the presence of General Dalbir Singh at Khulna's sprawling Circuit House Maidan, in front of thousands of local residents and hysterical *mukti*s begging Indian officers to hand over Hyat and his men to them for a few minutes. 'We will not kill them but shall teach them a few lessons that they will never forget.' The Indian officers displayed considerable patience and persuasive skill to calm them down. Thus, the curtains came down on the 13-day Indo-Pak conflict and the nine-month-long liberation war.

Since I was the only correspondent allowed to be present during Hyat-Dalbir's tête-à-tête, my Khulna surrender coverage caught the attention of many foreign correspondents, especially of Martin Woollacott of London's *The Guardian*. They had stationed themselves in Calcutta during the war. Woollacott came to the Statesman House to meet Sunanda K. Datta-Ray and requested him to convey his congratulations to me for my 'excellent Khulna coverage'. He had also taken the trouble of sending me a handwritten congratulatory message by post. That the liberation war would be over in less than nine months with the Mitra Bahini decisively winning a military victory in a 13-day war was an incredible experience not only for me but also for the most optimistic Bengalis.

Many Bengalis who had begun to harbour doubts about the fate of their *muktijuddho* were finally at peace. For months they were apprehensive that the war would continue aimlessly for an indefinite period and they would not be able to reach their goal. Never before in recent history had liberation wars achieved victory within a time span of nine months. It took Fidel Castro almost six years to overthrow the military dictator Batista from power in Cuba in a revolutionary war. That the dream of the majority of Bengalis of having a nation, a national flag and a national anthem of their own would translate into reality in such a short time benumbed them. It was too good to be true.

Many seemed unprepared for this historic and dramatic development. Even I was overcome with an overpowering sense of fulfilment; it was as if I had realized a goal that I had set out to achieve on 27 March, when I first went to the Petrapole border to report on the liberation war and decided to stand by the defenseless, persecuted and hapless Bengalis. Peter Hazelhurst, the South Asia correspondent of *The Times*, London, seeing my professional commitment to the liberation war coverage had commented to C.R. Irani, our managing director, 'Your Manash Ghosh has become a journalist turned *muktijoddha*.'

In less than a week's time I was to get the good news that my editor, N.J. Nanporia, 'was pleased to appoint me as *The Statesman's* bureau chief in Dacca'. He acknowledged my 'excellent coverage of Bangladesh's liberation war'. While handing over the appointment letter, he wished me luck and said that having reported death and destruction for the past nine months and also having seen from close quarters the birth pangs of a newborn nation, I would now be entering a new phase of reporting to focus on how a war-devastated Bangladesh would meet the challenges to rebuild and reboot itself on its way to recovery.

During the next three years of my posting in Dacca, I did exactly that.

Scene at Petrapole-Benapole border near Bongaon town as rally cars participating in the Second Asian Highway Car Rally roll across the Indo-East Pakistan border on 15 November 1970, heading for Dacca. Photo courtesy of Nikhil Bhattacharya

Streams of blood which flowed down the drain of a bathroom of a Pabna Industrial township flat where the Pak military had slaughtered the town's *muktijoddhas* and Awami League leaders following the 25 March crackdown. Photo courtesy of Shyamadas Basu

The first refugee arrivals from Bangladesh at India's Gede Railway Station on 27 March 1970. Photo courtesy of Shyamadas Basu

One of the many refugee camps that had mushroomed around Kalyani town to accommodate the ceaseless flow of refugees into India. Photo courtesy of Sudin Roy

This scene near the Tehatta border had brought tears to my eyes. The little girls who along with their mothers had no food for three days had their first morsel after they crossed over to India. The rice the two mothers had cooked for their daughters and themselves was not enough for all of them. So I saw the daughters crying. My office driver Mahboob went and bought 2 kg of rice and delivered it to the women for them to eat. The photo shows one of the mothers lighting the *chullah* or the makeshift oven to cook rice again. Photo courtesy of Shyamadas Basu

Author on extreme right while fleeing from Pabna along with its deputy commissioner Nurul Kader Khan and his personal security. Two of my *Statesman* colleagues Chandra Sekhar Sarkar (extreme left) and staff photographer Shyamadas Basu (on Nurul Kader's left) are also seen. Nurul Kader can be seen carrying his shot gun and his portable wireless set (partly visible). The photo was taken on the Padma river's vast *chawr* land just before boarding a rowboat. Photo courtesy of Shyamadas Basu

Major Abu Osman Chowdhury with his AK-47 rifle at his Chuadanga command headquarter. This photo was taken by the British Labour MP and a junior minister in Harold Wilson's government John Stonehouse in my presence. Photo courtesy of Abu Osman Chowdhury

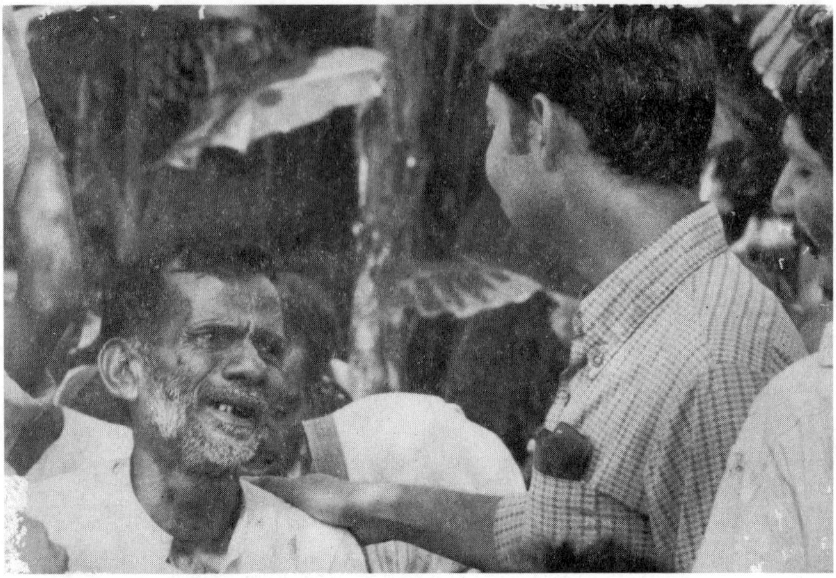

Author consoling a terrorized refugee family head who was in tears while narrating the atrocities his family faced at the hands of the Pak military just before crossing into India. Photo courtesy of Sudin Roy

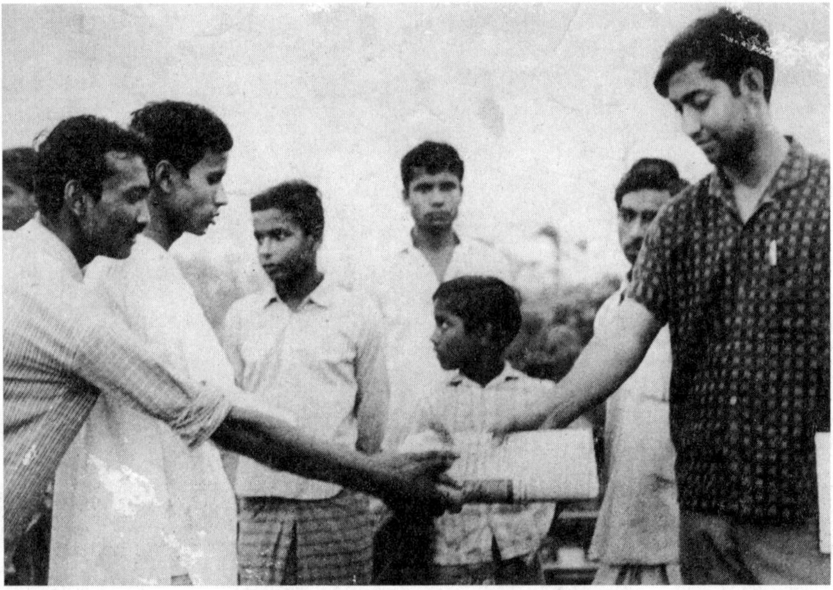

Author handing over copies of *The Statesman* to Darsana station railway staff after crossing into Bangladesh on the way to Chuadanga. Photo courtesy of Shyamadas Basu

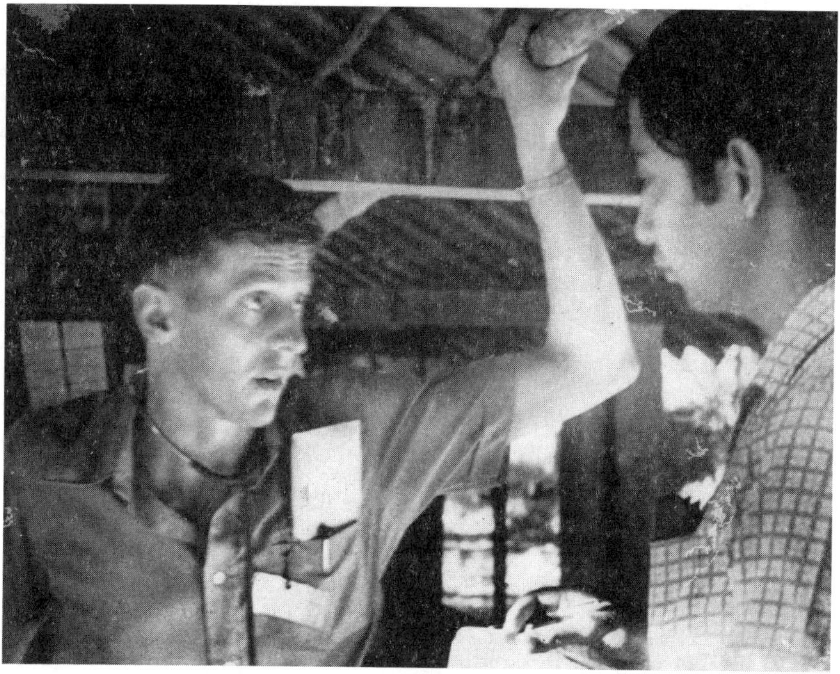

Author in conversation with a French doctor of Médecins Sans Frontières at the MSF field hospital in the Salt Lake refugee camp. Photo courtesy of Sudin Roy

Author learning target practice with an unarmed LMG at the Raiganj Mukti Bahini camp. Photo courtesy of Sudin Roy

Author with Captain K.N. Huda, sub sector commander of sector number eight in his Mukti Bahini camp in Kushtia. With his AK-47 rifle on his lap, he and his NCO are poring over a war map for launching a daring attack on a company of Pak Army's Jessore brigade in which he fought valiantly in early December. Photo courtesy of Sudin Roy

Graveyard of Pak Army's US-made Patton and Chaffee tanks at Garibpur after a fierce tank battle. Photo courtesy of Sudin Roy

Niyomito Bahini men with mortar, grenade launchers and rifles heading for the front in Khulna. Photo courtesy of Sudin Roy

The author at the helm of the boat which carried the *muktijoddhas* from the Ganga's Jalangi ghat to carry out a daring attack on the Sarda police academy in Rajshahi. Photo courtesy of Shyamadas Basu

ACKNOWLEDGEMENTS

This book could not have been written without the constant encouragement that my loving daughter Banshori provided while my wife and I were stuck in her Chennai home for almost one-and-a-half years because of the pandemic and the resultant lockdown. Banshori urged me to fruitfully utilize my time by writing this book which I had been planning for years. She would inspire me by saying 'pen down Bangladesh's birth by writing on the *muktijuddho*'. Fortunately, the relevant notes and books that I had taken with me to Chennai came in handy to undertake this bold venture. My granddaughter Avanti, a computer wizard, helped me retrieve my writings which I lost several times while storing them in various files. My wife Shelly would also encourage me to continue writing whenever I felt tired and listless. My friends and well-wishers Achin Roy, Anirban Chakravarty and Dilip Chakravarty would call me up to find out how much I had progressed in my work.

Once I had finished writing, I sent my manuscript to my former *Statesman* colleague Aditi Roy Ghatak for her feedback. She made some invaluable suggestions in restructuring certain chapters and their contents which I readily undertook. I profusely thank my former *Statesman* photographer colleagues Sudin Roy and Shyamadas Basu, both of whom unfortunately have passed away long ago, for having given me photographs, captured on their personal cameras, that they always carried with them, as their 'personal present and memento' for having accompanied me to various battlefronts. Also, I convey my sincere thanks to Dr Nirmal Kanti Bhattacharjee, Editorial Director of Niyogi Books, for readily agreeing to publish my work after hearing the broad outlines of my manuscript over the phone. Last but not the least, I express my deep sense of appreciation to the editor Sucharita Ghosh whose overall handling of my manuscript has been just exemplary.